D0122645

FRIENDS OF THE
SACRAMENTO
PUBLIC LIBRARY

THIS BOOK WAS DONATED BY
FRIENDS OF THE
MCKINLEY LIBRARY

The Sacramento Public Library gratefully acknowledges this
contribution to support and improve Library services in the community.

SACRAMENTO PUBLIC LIBRARY

When
I Was
White

A MEMOIR

Sarah Valentine

St. Martin's Press

New York

The Library of Congress Cataloging-in-Publication Data is available upon
request.

ISBN 978-1-250-14675-5 (hardcover)
ISBN 978-1-250-14676-2 (ebook)

First Edition: August 2019

10 9 8 7 6 5 4 3 2 1

To my past and future selves,
and to my family

Author's Note

Memory is imperfect, and I have truthfully portrayed the events and conversations described in the book to the best of my recollection. I recognize that others' memories of these events and conversations may differ from my own. To that end, some names and personal details have been changed or omitted to protect the identities of those portrayed in the book. I would like to thank my friends and family for being positive, supportive influences in my life.

In lieu of a public acknowledgment, I have chosen to thank all of the wonderful people involved in the creation and production of this book privately.

WHY SOME PEOPLE BE MAD AT ME SOMETIMES

they ask me to remember
but they want me to remember
their memories
and I keep on remembering
mine

—LUCILLE CLIFTON

When
I Was
White

One

On my first day of school, my mother dressed me in a red plaid dress with a white top and an apple-shaped pocket. She pulled my hair into neat, tight pigtails with red plastic balls on the hairbands. She held my yellow raincoat so I could push my arms through the sleeves and steadied my galoshes so I could place my feet into them one at a time, my hands holding onto her shoulders for support. She handed me my Wonder Woman lunch box. Inside were a carefully wrapped sandwich, fruit and a cookie, a thermos filled with hot chocolate, and a napkin on which she had colored a sunny scene with flowers and bluebirds. *You are my sunshine,* it read.

She drove me to the bus stop in our blue station wagon in the rain. Fall leaves littered the street, disappearing into deep puddles. The rain rushed down the sidewalk gutters into the grates below the street. Looking out the window, I wondered where the dark grates led.

"Where does all the water go?" I asked my mom, but she had her eyes on the road: my little brother Patrick, who had just turned one, was in a car seat in the back.

I was five. My dad, who was at work, was twenty-six. My mom, already a mother of two, was twenty-five.

When we arrived at the bus stop, my mom got out of the car and held an umbrella over my head. The school bus sat idling a few yards away, the exhaust rising in thick plumes.

She bent down, straightened my collar, and said, "Have fun. Be good. Don't miss me too much."

I was ready to go; I'd never ridden a school bus before.

The doors cranked open, and I turned to the waiting mystery, my first journey away from home. My mom grabbed my sleeve, and I turned back around.

"Remember, I love you," she said. "My little girl, my sunshine. I love you so much."

"I love you, too, Mommy!" I said and gave her a hug in my rain-slicked coat.

I ran onto the bus and waved to her out the window from my seat as we pulled away. Standing under the umbrella next to the station wagon, her hair long and brown, she waved back.

I couldn't see that her eyes were filled with tears.

Two

We went to Catholic school, got dressed for church every Sunday.

St. Alexis, named for the patron saint of beggars, was a plain church with a school, orchard playground, rectory, and convent, all situated around a parking lot that doubled as our kickball field. A statue of the Virgin Mary greeted you when you drove up the winding tree-lined road and entered the church grounds.

The whole town of Wexford was like that: winding and tree-lined. It sat in the North Hills of Pittsburgh, a suburb of gray skies, car dealerships, and graveyards but also of rolling hills, green lawns, and fireworks in July.

We lived in a cozy town house in a neighborhood called Hickory Hills that bordered the woods. Pat and I had our own bedrooms, and when my youngest brother, Tommy, was born, he slept in a crib next to my parents' bed. I had fun chasing our cat, Kitty, into the converted garage basement, until she ran behind the furnace, which was blocked by my dad's old weight bench. Running down the steep hill across the street revealed a park surrounded by maple groves.

From the highest point on the swing I could see the tops of the trees that disappeared into the ravine below.

St. Teresa of Avila, St. Sebastian's, and St. Alphonsus were all located in the North Hills, but my parents picked our neighborhood because it was closest to St. Alexis. Maybe they liked its humble patron, or maybe they liked that the school had an accelerated learning program that was intended to be college preparatory. The church was originally built to be the school gymnasium, so it was flat, rectangular, and unadorned. But the back wall had been replaced with glass and gave on to a stand of pines behind the church. Above the altar, a larger-than-life crucifix hung from the ceiling, contrasting the view of tranquility with a portrait of grim death.

Father Rogers founded St. Alexis in the 1970s. He was a gruff older man who sped through the Apostles' Creed and kept his homilies short so his parishioners could get home in time to watch the Steelers play on Sunday. The services of the younger priest, Father Kunkel, were more thoughtful, and he took time to talk to the parents after mass. Five nuns, the Sisters of the Holy Spirit, lived in the convent. They, along with a handful of laywomen, were our schoolteachers.

My mom was one of the nuns' favorite parents. She baked banana bread and zucchini bread that she gave me to drop off at the convent.

"Tell your mother I said thank you," said Sister Stephanie, my first-grade teacher. Then she leaned down closer. "But don't tell her the braided loaf she gave us was raw on the inside!"

I liked Sister Stephanie. She had a kind, round face that beamed with mischief under her veil. I didn't like Sister Anselm, who would become my fourth-grade teacher. With a pinched face and small round glasses on the end of her nose, she bristled with righteous disapproval.

One day when she was visiting the other classrooms, she leaned over my desk and asked, "What are you drawing?"

I showed her my drawing of a fluffy cat that I thought was quite lifelike.

She drew back and made a noise of disgust. Then she took the drawing and put it on her desk, which meant I was never going to get it back. I was confused by her reaction until Sister Stephanie came over to reassure me.

"She thinks cats are the devil's children," she said with a wink.

When I was at St. Alexis, I wanted to be a nun. Except for crotchety Sister Anselm, they seemed sweet and serene. Their long black-and-white robes, the black veils edged in white intrigued me, like they were part of a secret order and knew something we didn't. Our school did not endorse corporal punishment, so I never experienced the ruler or stick that was common in stories about Catholic school.

On Friday mornings we attended mass. After communion, Father Rogers gave a short homily.

"Strive to be like Mary," he said. "For she was without sin and submitted to God's will."

We bowed our heads in silent prayer, supposedly to ask Mary for her guidance. I pictured the Virgin in her white veil, blue cape, and white tunic, a golden halo rising from her head. She had long brown hair like my mom.

I thought about the Holy Spirit, which I pictured as a white bird on fire that brought holiness and grace. Because they were named for it, I figured the sisters had the magic bird locked up somewhere in the convent.

I knew Jesus died for our sins. I didn't entirely understand what that meant, but I felt like I owed him a great deal. I knew from reciting the stations of the cross that he was persecuted unjustly. That was partly why I wanted to become a nun; how else could I ever repay my debt and right that eternal wrong?

I pictured God as a man in the clouds. He was everyone's father, but especially Jesus's and was always watching, like Santa Claus.

I didn't understand how God made Mary pregnant through the Holy Spirit or how Joseph was Jesus's earthly father. How could a spirit make you pregnant? How could you have two fathers—one you knew and one you didn't?

"In the name of the Father, the Son, and the Holy Spirit. Amen," Father Rogers concluded. We crossed ourselves and when the service ended we filed out of the church.

The line back to class was the best time to practice our swears, which we traded like our own secret knowledge and whispered to each other when the nuns weren't looking.

"I know the worst one," Jenny Ross said.

"What is it?" I asked. We already knew *damn* and *hell*, but that was kind of the teachers' fault because they taught us those in religion class. I already knew some other colorful phrases, but I was curious about what Jenny had to reveal. I leaned closer.

"Butt lick!" she said triumphantly. I gasped. I'd never heard that one before and immediately began to think of all the people I could call a *butt lick* at recess.

With short black hair and freckles, Jenny reminded me of Punky Brewster and was always getting in trouble. I called her Punky and she called me Cherie, who was Punky's best friend on the show. I didn't really get it because I didn't think I looked like Cherie, a brown girl with her hair combed into neat, tight pigtails. I let it go because it meant I was Jenny's best friend.

Our moms were also friends. Sometimes after school, we would stop by their house, and she and Mrs. Ross would talk in the kitchen while we played in Jenny's room. The Rosses were from the South, and Mrs. Ross insisted I call her Miss Patty. It felt exotic to call a grown-up by her first name, especially my friend's mom. Miss Patty spoke with a sassy twang, and I saw where Jenny got her spirit. I think my mom was in awe of her, too. She talked about how fit Miss Patty was, how she ran around the high school every day. While I was the oldest of three, Jenny was the youngest. Her older sister listened to the Grateful Dead, and her brother listened to rap and played football. We'd sneak into both of their rooms, portals into danger and excitement. I was entranced by the Run-DMC poster on her brother's wall and the skull with a crown of roses on her sister's.

One day Jenny invited me over with another one of her friends, Emily, who was African American. Emily and I were friends, but not best friends, and it annoyed me that parents and teachers often confused our names. *I don't even look like her*, I would think. Jenny was my best friend, and I thought it made more sense to confuse the names of two people who were always together, not those of two people who weren't.

I didn't know much about race, but I knew it existed; I thought some people were black, but most people were normal. I knew, for example, that Run-DMC and most other rappers were black, and I knew that my family and I were not. I couldn't explain why, but to me, being black made Emily seem different. Her family lived in a bigger house than any of ours. Her father was handsome and kind, and her mother reminded me of one of the elegant ladies on a soap opera. They were fancier than we were, which I felt put them in a higher class, but they were also black, which put them in a different category altogether.

While we were playing, Emily got a nosebleed and ran to the bathroom. I peered around the open door, my face half reflected in the bathroom mirror. I stood transfixed as I wondered what color her blood would be when it came pouring out of her nose. *She's not like the rest of us,* I thought. *Surely her blood would be a different color, too.* Such an important difference had to be more than skin-deep. When her bright red blood stained the white towel in her hands, I slid away from the door.

Three

In sixth grade, I moved to Carson Middle School, and the girl who wanted to be pure like the Virgin Mary grew into the teenager who wanted to dance like MC Hammer. Instead of wearing tight pigtails, I wore my hair down in all its frizzy glory and earned the nickname "Slash," though I pulled it back into a ponytail when I was around my mom.

Jenny and I were still friends, but not best friends. Although I was out of Catholic school, I was still in the Girl Scouts. Jenny quit in fifth grade, calling it "lame," but I stayed on, doing crafts, going camping, and earning merit badges. Dressed in my green uniform, I went door-to-door with my mom to sell cookies. I was not a good salesperson; I hated going up to strangers' doors. Eventually, my dad just took the sign-up form to work and came back with a page full of orders. My family always ordered a dozen, and my favorite part about Girl Scouts was opening the brightly colored boxes, pulling out the long sleeves of Thin Mints and sliding out the plastic trays of Samoas.

Not long after Tommy was born, we moved out of Hickory Hills to a three-bedroom house on Lincoln Boulevard with two white columns and a row of hedges in front. The neighborhood was known as the Presidentials, with Roosevelt Street, Taft Place, and Van Buren Lane making up our plan. Now we each had our own rooms. Pat's room had the Nintendo, the computer, and a trundle bed with a choo-choo train comforter. Tommy's room had white wallpaper with red, blue, and yellow stars, a deep blue carpet, and glow-in-the-dark stars on the ceiling. His tall white cabinet was the same one I'd had when I was a baby. My room had white and yellow princess furniture with brass handles on the dresser drawers, a canopy bed, and a rolltop desk. It was also a good place for hiding things, or so I thought.

The living room with its big floral couches and high-backed green armchair was for special occasions only. The TV room had a woodsy theme and the couches were made of nubby fabric that could better stand up to kids. The couch frame, coffee table, and dining table were all oak, with hard corners. If you bumped your elbow, stubbed your toe, or hit your head because you were roughhousing, it was your own fault.

In addition to our tortoiseshell Kitty, we got Knight, a black Labrador retriever. My mom had a black Lab named Mother when she was a kid. She laughed recalling her parents yelling, "Mother! Get off the bed!" and how funny it must have sounded to outsiders when she told her parents, "Mother peed on the floor again!" Mother the black Lab seemed to be one of the only happy memories my mom had of her childhood and we decided to carry on the tradition. We went to a breeder's house and picked Knight out of a litter of puppies. His purebred certificate from the American Kennel Club listed the full name we gave him, Sir William of Wexford, along with his parents' names. His mother, Athena, was a sleek, muscular black Lab, and his father, Old Yellow Thor, was a hulking yellow Lab who had sired multiple litters. With such a pedigree, Knight was destined to be a mighty beast.

Knight was only a few months old when we brought him home, the same age as Tommy, and as one grew so did the other. By the time Tommy was four, Knight was a 115-pound terror and taller than I was standing on his hind legs. He thought he was above the children in the household hierarchy. He was kicked out of every obedience class that my mother took him to. When he was around one year old, she took him to a class in North Park, where woods and picnic groves ringed a lake. As soon as he saw the water, Knight broke off from his leash, charged toward the lake and jumped in, swimming away to his heart's delight while the other dogs sat patiently, quivering at the temptation of freedom but not daring to disobey their masters. Knight eventually came back to shore, muddy, wet, and self-satisfied. That was the beginning of the end of his training journey, and because we failed to control him then, we'd felt it was impossible to do so now.

When we were twelve, Jenny and I played clowns at my brother Patrick's eighth birthday party. My mom sewed two patchwork clown costumes complete with red, white, and blue pompoms on the chests. We got rainbow wigs and sticks of grease paint. Thick white covered our faces; we drew red clown lips around our own and blue ovals around our eyes. I made little red hearts on my cheeks. Jenny decided to paint sharp blue triangles around her eyes, making her look a bit like John Wayne Gacy. She got a bunch of party hats and strapped them all over her wig.

"I'm Horny the Clown!" she said.

My parents had planned Patrick's eighth birthday party to be a big event. The kitchen, yard, and driveway were decorated with crepe paper and balloons. Jenny and I led the kids in decorating paper plates to make clown faces that they glued to popsicle sticks. Everyone got a can of Silly String. My dad had the video camera out and recorded Pat enjoying his surprise gift, a red battery-powered Power Wheels Jeep. Pat rode it around the sloping drive-way singing, *Pow-pow Power Wheels! Pow-pow Power Wheels! Power Wheels—Power makes it go!* His friends screamed with envy and glee.

Just then, we heard another scream from the kitchen. My mom had gone to bring out the cake, but while we were all outside, Knight had jumped up, put his big paws on the kitchen counter, and reached his head into the cake box like a shark. When we ran in to see what happened, we saw my mom standing dumbfounded in front of a torn box and mangled cake all over the floor. Knight was ban-ished to the basement, and we heard him whining and barking and scratching at the door. Gathering herself, my mom herded us all back outside to play games so my dad could run to the Giant Eagle to pick up cupcakes and some more candles.

The next week, Jenny invited me to her house. It was summer, and the air was thick with honeysuckle. We walked down her drive-way and rounded the corner, down a street that led to a part of the neighborhood hidden by trees.

There were smaller houses here, not like her big house that sat on a hill. They were single-story, closer together, and some were sepa-rated by chain-link fences.

We walked up to a house with red siding. A dog barked, and I hung back. Jenny led the way through the chain-link gate and knocked on the door.

A kid about our age answered. He was tall, tan like me, and a little bit chubby. He had wavy black hair; his eyes and nose somehow looked different. I thought he was cute. He yanked the collar of the wild Pekingese that danced and yelped around his legs.

"Get down, Molly!" he said, maneuvering it behind the door.

"Hey, Jenny," he said. I wondered if he even knew I was there.

"Hey, Rich," Jenny said. Then, as if remembering, said: "This is my friend Sarah."

Rich looked at me, and I couldn't tell what he was thinking. It made me shy, and I pretended like I didn't know if he was there, either.

We hung out in Rich's backyard, which had an aboveground pool. We didn't have our swimsuits, so we just sat in the grass behind the honeysuckle bushes.

"You know you can drink them," Jenny said, plucking one of the small white trumpets. "They taste like honey."

We all tried it. I couldn't taste anything, and anyway, the stamens tickled my nose. I had to wave away bees and eventually gave up.

"Oh yeah, it's great!" I said, pretending to take a big swig. Rich laughed, and I beamed, knowing he'd noticed me. Then he picked one and threw his head back, pretending to take a swig, too, and then we were all swigging, picking blossoms, getting drunk on honeysuckle.

In middle school, I grew to my full height, and my coordination improved. In softball, I went from being an awkward right fielder to an athletic first baseman. In basketball, I went from being a kid more interested in exploring the locker room with my friends to a star forward, sprinting down the court for layups. With my parents' encouragement, I began to practice every day and coaches began to notice.

Boys started to notice me, too. I would see Douglas Bradford, who was a year older than I, suddenly creep up next to me in the hall. We knew he was adopted because the older white lady, more like a grandmother, who showed up with him at church could not have been his mom. He hung out with his white friend Chad, who wore sideways caps and basketball jerseys.

One day, Douglas and Chad came up to me while I was at my locker. Chad nudged Douglas, who took out a small piece of paper and in a nervous voice read, "Sarah, you have a vol-up-tu-ous ass."

I rolled my eyes and stalked away. Douglas didn't talk to me after that, though I still saw him peering at me in the halls and cafeteria. Meanwhile, I had my eye on Bobby Jones, an eighth grader with blond hair, rosy cheeks, and bright blue eyes. He smiled at me and said, "Hey," in the halls, but the girls he talked to at their lockers were blond like him.

Rich and I became friends. We even had nicknames for each other.

"Hey, Oreo!" I'd say if I passed him in the hall.

"Hey, Hydrox!" he'd yell back. It was an insult to be called the Brand X version of Oreos, so sometimes I made sure to call him that first.

Jenny told me one of Rich's parents was black. We went over to his house a few more times, but the only other member of the household I met was Molly. I didn't tell my parents about my Rich. He wasn't a bad kid, but he was a year older than I was, and we didn't know his parents. Something told me to keep our friendship a secret.

But it was a good secret. When he attended my middle school basketball games and shouted, "Oreo!" from the stands, I thought nobody knew what it meant but me.

Four

The Intermediate was our school district's name for the building that housed the ninth and tenth grades. The senior high was a bigger building, for eleventh and twelfth graders. In middle school, we dreamed of "move-up day," the day we got to visit the Intermediate to see what our first year of high school would be like.

Jenny and I grew apart by ninth grade, but the students from two middle schools, Carson and Ingomar, were coming together into one building, and that meant I would meet some new friends.

I met Tara and Abby in Mr. Yanzek's English class.

At the beginning of our first class, Mr. Yanzek told us to take out a piece of paper.

"Write this down," he said, and he rattled off a list: "Lil E. Tee. Casual Lies. Dance Floor."

We wrote diligently, but when he got to *Dance Floor,* we stopped and looked up at him.

"Do you know what you're writing?" he bellowed from beneath his mustache. "It's a list of the horses that won the Kentucky Derby last year. Now crumple those papers up and throw them in the trash."

We crumpled our papers up and threw them at the wastebasket near his desk. It seemed like he was trying to teach us a lesson, but he never told us what it was.

"Hey," he said to the girl sitting in front of me. "What's your name?"

"Tara," she said.

"Tara, why are you wearing hiking boots with that skirt?"

I looked down. The girl in front of me was wearing a white sweater and a long black-and-blue plaid wool skirt with Timberland boots. She had blond streaks in her hair. She looked so cool.

"Uh, because I want to," she said.

Oh my God, she is so cool, I thought. I never dreamed of talking back to a teacher, even one as strange as Mr. Yanzek.

"Good. That's good," he said, and then he gave us a vocab quiz.

After class, I saw Tara at her locker. Two other girls were standing with her. They were tall and pretty.

"Hey," I said. "That was pretty weird, right?"

"Yeah," said Tara. "I can't believe he made us write down the names of those horses. You're really good at vocab though."

"Whatever," I said, but I was thrilled that she noticed.

"I only got a 98," said Abby, who sat behind me in class. She had a neatly trimmed brown bob, her bangs pulled back with a barrette. Tara and Abby had gone to Ingomar Middle School together.

"Same here," said Tara. "Does anyone even know what a *fo'c'sle* is?"

I did because I had already read *Moby-Dick,* but I wasn't going to say anything.

"I had Mr. Mossel," the third girl, Courtney, said. "For the whole class he just talked about the genius of Jonathan Swift."

I recognized Courtney from a fun run we'd had through North

Park in middle school. There was a lanky girl with dark blond hair at the front of the pack with me as we ran through the muddy woods. She and Tara both went to St. Teresa's. Abby didn't go to church because she was half Jewish. She explained that her mom was Catholic and her dad was Jewish, so she celebrated both Hanukkah and Christmas. I didn't know someone could have half of their identity be different than the other half, and this gave Abby a certain mystique.

My friends and I related to the world through inside jokes. Now when we saw each other in the hall, we would yell:

"Casual Lies!"

"Dance Floor!"

"Fo'c'sle!"

We ended up in World Cultures class together, our curriculum's only course on the non-Western world.

As teenagers growing up in the North Hills in the 1990s, we thought we were the center of civilization. I was savvy in art, English, history, and math, but when it came to learning about South America, Africa, and the Middle East, my friends and I just thought it was a joke. Foreign places had crazy names:

Turkey?

Yemen?

The Strait of Hormuz?

The Strait of Hormuz?

The people of these cultures spoke hilarious languages and dressed like clowns. The world of World Cultures was too inconceivably different from our own for us to take it seriously. Growing up in a small corner of America, we thought all people lived as we did, and if they didn't, it meant that they were underdeveloped and needed to be shown the way.

After we started taking World Cultures class, instead of playing shirts versus skins at the YMCA, my guy friends and I would play Sunnis versus Shiites. The Shiites, being the more militant group, would take off their T-shirts and tie them around their heads. We'd add commentary like *Markovich dribbles down the court, Thomson is covering Markovich, but Thomson's T-shirt falls off his head and Markovich takes it in for a layup. Sunnis win 5–0.*

This was the extent to which we understood world cultures.

Our teacher, Mr. Lynch, was tall, pasty, and balding. He wore '70s glasses, thin shirts that showed the outline of the undershirts beneath, and brown polyester pants that sat too high on his waist. His awkward manner only served to make the class seem more absurd. He had a slight lisp, and my friends and I would die with suppressed laughter when he pronounced words like *muezzin, imam, wa,* and *shibumi.*

He had traveled to Nigeria, but even this we didn't take seriously.

What was Nigeria?

He talked about participating in the kola nut ceremony and how much he sweated when he had to eat the spicy sauce and kola nut that were part of the welcoming ritual for guests.

All we heard was "cola nut" and pictured Mr. Lynch drinking a Coke filled with nuts and sweating.

"Oh, these cola nuts are spicy! Oh! Cola nuts!" we'd say, mimicking his voice.

I realized years later that Mr. Lynch must have loved what he taught in order to put up with our ignorance. He probably traveled more than most of us ever would, but he was an unfortunate character in the play of our lives and couldn't contend with our desire to turn everything we didn't understand into humor. If someone had told us our behavior was offensive, I would have been shocked. I thought we were all "good kids," living the way our families and culture wanted us to.

Just before Thanksgiving, Mr. Lynch brought a guest to class, a friend he had met through his travels. Mr. Lynch's intention was to make the seemingly make-believe cultures of the world realer, but we were not ready to meet difference on equal terms.

A dark-skinned man walked into the room. He wore a loose-fitting shirt, matching pants, and cap. His clothes were brightly colored and patterned, and he painted a bizarre picture next to Mr. Lynch's blandness. We had no idea what to make of this stranger; he might as well have been from outer space.

"Class, this is Buba," Mr. Lynch said, with an emphasis on pronouncing the name *Boo-ba*. "He has been generous enough to come to our school. Please make him feel welcome."

Standing in front of the class, Buba told us that he was Nigerian. We didn't get much after that, as simply trying to take him in was already too much. He smiled as he spoke, much more at ease than we were. I had never seen or met anyone like him.

I was jolted back to attention when Buba held up a large swath of shimmering pink-and-gold fabric that he said women in Nigeria wore. At that moment, his eyes fell on me. Mr. Lynch noticed and called me to the front of the room to help demonstrate how it was worn.

At this, my classmates and I laughed openly, and it seemed in good fun. He would give us epic stories to tell later.

I stood between Buba and Mr. Lynch at the front of the class, facing the room, trying desperately to keep a straight face. As instructed, I stood still, my arms raised to the sides, as Buba wrapped the stiff cloth in a snakelike fashion around my body. I was wearing bulky jeans, a sweater, and sneakers, and as the fabric wound higher and higher around my body, finally draping the excess over my shoulder, I began to feel self-conscious. Buba was explaining the elements of traditional garb to the class, turning me this way and that as if I were a living exhibit.

Suddenly, I was too warm in all that fabric. With the eyes of the class on me, I could hear the snickering, the whispers; even Abby, Tara, and Courtney joined in. Part of me dismissed it as coincidence; they could have chosen anyone in the room. But another, deeper part of me realized it was something more.

I saw a sea of white faces looking me up and down, recording every detail, but this time I was not in on the joke.

This time I was the "other," and the joke was on me.

Five

As I grew into my teenage self, my difference felt like a kind of rebellion. My mother and I argued all the time, and I fixated on race as a taboo and inflammatory subject.

One night after dinner, I sat down with my family for another weekly ritual, watching *Married . . . with Children*. Al Bundy sat on the couch with his iconic scowl and a beer in his hand. Peg Bundy teetered in on high heels with her signature red bouffant, tight pants, and pushed-up cleavage to harangue Al in a shrill voice, and Kelly Bundy came down the stairs with bleach-blond hair and a miniskirt to the hoots and cheers of the audience. I never thought about the stereotypes or misogyny I saw onscreen; it was just another comedy.

The new, edgy hit show was *In Living Color*. With a nearly all-black cast and a team of Fly Girls, it was something I had never seen before. It came on after *Married . . . with Children*, a prime-time slot. "What is this?" My mother frowned the first time we watched, getting ready to change the channel.

"No!" I yelled. "It's *In Living Color*! I want to watch it!" She put the remote down as one of the Wayans brothers in a suit and tie impersonated a white person with a nasal voice and square demeanor.

"See," my mom said, "they *can* talk normally, so why don't they? Shows like this set a bad example. And why are there so many of them on TV?" she continued. "They're only 10 percent of the population but they're on every channel. It's not fair, don't you think?"

I had just learned about segregation in school, and though my family didn't drive through the city of Pittsburgh often, when we did, I noticed crumbling town houses with broken and boarded-up windows, sidewalks and front stoops populated with people of all ages, none of them white. I saw men and women in suits, too, driving nice cars and living in suburban neighborhoods like we did, but it was a stark contrast to what I saw in the city. It occurred to me that things were not all that different since the days of enforced segregation.

We didn't use separate drinking fountains or have to sit in different sections of the restaurant, but with a few exceptions, black people seemed to live in one part of town, white people in another.

"What do you know about it?" I yelled at my mom. "You never had to deal with slavery or segregation!"

"People aren't poor because of slavery or segregation," she said with the conviction of someone who knows she is right. "That's all in the past. People are poor because it's easier to collect food stamps than to work hard and get a job, and because shows like this make being poor in the ghetto seem cool."

I was rebelling against what I saw as my parents' bourgeois suburban values, even as I relied on them for support. It never occurred to me to financially cut myself off or that living under their roof was in itself an endorsement of those values. They were my parents, I thought. They were supposed to take care of me, no matter what. My concern for those I saw as less fortunate was the self-interested hypocrisy of privilege: claiming to defend people I really knew nothing about.

"It affects so few people," my mother would say. By *it*, she meant race. "We live in a democracy—majority rules!"

That wasn't the definition of democracy I had learned in school; I didn't think "majority rule" meant that the majority of the population got all the rights and everyone else had to fend for themselves, but somehow her point of view was impossible to argue with. During these arguments, she would conclude that even if racial discrimination did exist, it was not our problem.

Soon I discovered *Yo! MTV Raps,* which provided another window into an urban world I only saw on TV. I marveled at the Ed Lover dance. How did he make his body move in that way? I saw Run-DMC's jumpsuits, hats, chains, and sunglasses. They held their mics upside down and yelled words that had to be bleeped out. The sound of a record being scratched; break-dancers surrounded by cheering crowds against a backdrop of gray high-rises; Kangols; girls with big gold earrings and guys with big gold chains. I watched the Fresh Prince take the keys to the brand-new Porsche, its red curves as tight and sleek as the dress on the girl beside him.

I get it, I thought. *Parents just don't understand.*

When my mother insisted I couldn't watch *Yo! MTV Raps,* I'd stomp upstairs to my room and slam my door. In my bedroom full of stuffed animals and seashells, I'd flop down on my bed and play my cassette tapes: Bell Biv DeVoe, Boyz II Men, Candyman, Digital Underground. I turned to *Video Jukebox* on my little TV that sat on a white scalloped dresser and watched call-in request music videos through the static; I pulled the antennas left and right, but as hard as I tried, I never got a clear picture.

Around this time a kid named Brian asked me to a school dance.

"What happened at school today?" my mom asked me as she always did when I came home. I plopped my backpack down on the kitchen table.

"Not much," I said. "This kid wants to go to the dance with me."

"Really?" she asked, suddenly interested. I was a tomboy, and my mother always jumped at the chance for me to engage in more feminine activities. Getting dressed up and attending a school dance with a nice young man was definitely one of those things. Plus, she knew I was well liked by my peers but had missed out on being asked to other dances. It bothered me more than I let on, but she still saw it; all the guys with whom I hung out, played basketball and tennis, asked flirtier, blonder, more petite girls to dances when the time came.

"What's his name?" she asked. I told her, and she proceeded to ask what he was like.

"He plays soccer . . . he's kind of a nerd. I think his dad's a doctor." She could tell I wasn't enthused about the prospect, but she wanted to encourage me.

One of the reasons I was not excited was that Brian was so shy that he'd had a mutual friend, Kristen, ask me out for him. Kristen and I were friendly but didn't talk much. In the preceding weeks, however, she'd made a point to strike up conversations with me and ask me personal questions like what was my favorite color and favorite flower.

Since I had no idea where these questions were coming from, and since I'm contrary by nature, I'd answered, "Brown," and "I don't like flowers." Little had I known she'd been passing this intelligence along to Brian, who apparently wanted to impress me with just the right corsage. When she finally asked me to the dance on Brian's behalf, I said a tentative "Yes," mainly because Kristen was popular and genuinely friendly. I thought, *Well, if she and Brian are friends, he can't be that bad.*

When my mother asked me what he looked like, I replied: "Okay."

It was the most accurate description I could think of; Brian was neither attractive nor unattractive, of average height and build with no outstanding features.

Somehow my mother found out that Brian was black, and her attitude about my going to the dance with him changed completely. The next day when I got home from school, she confronted me.

"You didn't tell me he was black," she said.

"I didn't think it mattered," I replied.

"Well, you're not going to the dance with him."

"Why?" I yelled. "Because he's, like, the only black kid in our class?"

"Let someone else go with the only black kid in your class," my mom said.

My mom made me tell Brian, which I did through Kristen, that I had a basketball program to attend on the day of the dance. I did have a program, but it was early in the day and wouldn't have interfered.

The night of the dance, a friend's mom took some of the other of my friends and me to tour the brand-new Pittsburgh International Airport. We marveled at the glossy, high-end retail stores with handbags and high-heeled shoes in the windows. It was the first time I'd ever seen people movers, and we rode these back and forth until my friend's mom told us it was time to go home.

I wasn't upset about not going to the dance with Brian, since we hardly knew each other; I was upset on principle. When I argued with my mother about race and injustice, she insisted that race was "made up." But in the case of my going to the dance with Brian, she acted as if it were deadly real.

Six

When I was sixteen, we moved from the house on Lincoln Boulevard to a much larger house on Ash Court, a cul-de-sac in a newly developed part of town. We didn't have enough furniture to fill all the rooms, and though the birthday parties and holiday celebrations continued, the cavernous house with a chandelier hanging from the high ceiling in the entranceway didn't really feel like home. But it meant my dad was doing well and that he could take care of us, which was all he ever wanted.

I played volleyball in the fall, basketball in the winter, and ran track in the spring.

My brothers played baseball, basketball, and, most importantly, football.

On Friday nights, my friends and I went to the varsity football games. No weather could keep us away; if it was cold we brought blankets, if it rained we wore ponchos. We'd giggle and whisper about the boys we liked, cheer for our team, and boo the refs. We developed elaborate schemes for getting the attention of senior boys, on which we never followed through. Afterward, we'd go to Pizza

Roma, eat giant, greasy slices of pizza, drink Cokes, and continue our scheming.

I drove my family's old blue Buick station wagon that had a rear-facing seat in the back. My friends and I blasted classic rock and disco from its small speakers and called it the double Dutch bus. We crammed in as many of us as we could, and after Pizza Roma, a handful of us would go to an all-night diner—usually King's, Eat'n Park, or Denny's—to drink coffee, eat sundaes, and complain about how much life in suburbia sucked.

That summer I began working at King's Family Restaurant. It was a grimy diner with country décor that sat right off the freeway. Folks wore their good jeans to King's, and the most popular item on the menu was Salisbury steak. King's was known for its ice cream bar, and Little League teams would come in after their games to try to conquer the King's Castle, a twenty-four-scoop sundae with nuts, bananas, chocolate, peanut butter and caramel sauce, whipped cream, and maraschino cherries. It came in a red plastic castle, and if you finished it, the castle was yours.

After my shifts serving taco salad, liver and onions, iceberg lettuce salads, and soups of the day, I'd lie on the hood of the station wagon eating leftovers out of a to-go container. I'd look up at the stars and fantasize about leaving. I couldn't wait to go to college and get out of Wexford. I didn't care where; I just wanted it to be somewhere far away. Even though I excelled in all the ways that counted in my high school, I felt different from most people. I looked different, cared about and noticed different things. I saw letters, numbers, and music in color. When I mentioned this to my friends, Tara asked:

"Do all words have colors?"

"Yes," I said.

"What color is butt plug?"

"Blue and orange," I replied.

I was often sad when I was alone. Mostly, I kept the things that made me different to myself. It was good to be smart, but not weird. It was good to be tan, but not dark-skinned. It was good to be mentally tough, but not emotional. I learned to cover my introversion by throwing big parties. I don't know how much I consciously understood these things, but they were etched into my subconscious as clearly as if someone had written them there.

I realized, with the encouragement of one of my English teachers, that I wanted to be a writer. In my fantasies, I lived in New York City and traveled the world, writing about my discoveries and adventures. I would be like Larry Darrell in *The Razor's Edge,* or Jack Kerouac in *On the Road,* except I wouldn't be as whiny. I never thought I'd write about my own life. None of the great works of literature we read in high school were about teenage girls growing up in the suburbs. None were about teenage girls at all. The books about women we did read were *The Scarlet Letter, The Awakening, The Bell Jar, Hedda Gabler, Wuthering Heights,* and *Tess of the D'Urbervilles.* Things never worked out well for the women in these stories; in fact, they all ended up spiritually or literally dead. I didn't see myself as a tragic flower wilting under the weight of the cruel world. The future I saw for myself was active and free, like a man's. I never thought to write about my own life because, according the literature I'd read, it wasn't worth writing about.

One day in English class, we were asked to write an in-class essay on the poem "One Art" by Elizabeth Bishop.

When I read this poem, it made me angry. I didn't understand why, but something in the poem hit a raw nerve. Most of the wisdom my parents and coaches instilled in me was about how to be a winner. What was the "art of losing"? Who would want to master that?

The villanelle's jaunty rhymes made it seem almost like a joke. I usually liked humor and irony, but the refrain had an ominous undertone I couldn't grasp.

I was used to understanding literature, but "One Art" elicited unwelcome confusion. I'd never lost anyone close to me; no family member had suffered any major trauma. My life in Wexford seemed to be without incident, protected and supported, just like my parents wanted. I'd always pushed away anger and sadness. But I couldn't hide the irritation I felt reading this poem. I hated it as I'd never hated anything before. I didn't know what loss was, or that I might be mourning something I didn't understand, but the feelings I kept inside were beginning to come out. Something huge and messy was about to break through, and it felt like disaster.

Meanwhile, my calendar was filled with activities to impress the college admissions boards. Tara, Courtney, and I volunteered at the Carnegie Science Center on the weekends, giving out flyers and greeting patrons at the entrance, giving tours of the model train exhibit, and pretending not to notice as our supervisor looked down our shirts or let his hand graze the backs of our pants. I was an honors and AP student but was also supposed to remain a three-sport athlete. When I quit the volleyball and track teams my senior year, my mother got angry.

"Why are you throwing your future away? You won't even remember this!" she said about the days I came home late after spending time with my friends instead of training. Whenever I complained about being pushed too hard, my mother would respond, "I wish someone had taken an interest in my future when I was growing up. I wish someone would have helped me apply for college or given me some kind of advice."

She recounted graduating from a Catholic high school in her small town and having no idea what to do next. Neither of her parents went to college, and even though my mother was a good student, they did not encourage her or take the time to learn about her interests.

In the end, she applied to community college because that's what her friend Karen was doing. When it came time for her to leave, her dad didn't even offer to drive her; she had to get a ride from Karen.

From that perspective, her over-parenting made sense. I had to follow all my interests, both academic and extracurricular, to the extreme. My schedule was always full. I took the SATs in seventh grade so I could start preparing early for the real thing. All of this fueled my success, but it also produced a feeling of pressure that never let up.

Things were different for my brothers. In high school, Pat rebelled and, despite receiving a perfect score on the SATs, he almost failed out of high school. Tom was a good student but only did what he needed to do to get by. When I protested that I was being made to do things my brothers didn't have to, my mom replied, "It's a man's world. Tommy and Pat will be fine. You have to try harder."

When I got a C in physics my senior year, my mother asked me, "Are you even serious about going to college? Why don't you sign up for Hills College right now, because you'll never get into Princeton with those grades."

"Hills College" was the community college of Allegheny County, located in the building where the Hills Department Store used to be. I didn't know if my mother regretted her own experience with community college, but "Hills College" became a euphemism in our family for falling short or giving up. I didn't want to end up there, but I didn't know where I wanted to go. I applied to Ivy League schools because that's what my parents wanted.

"It's my dream for you to go to Princeton," my mother would say. It sounded like the right goal to have, so it became my dream, too.

I was captain of the basketball team my senior year. My friends came to cheer me on, Tara and Courtney wearing their fiesta dresses because they had just gotten off from work at Chi-Chi's.

We always made it to state finals, and I wore my four-year letter jacket proudly. My brothers kept track of my defensive and offensive stats. Sometimes there were college scouts in the stands, and my parents were counting on my getting a full ride to play basketball at a good school.

Even though my parents were doing well financially, college was expensive, and they also had my brothers to think about. I played the best I could my senior year, but my heart wasn't in it. I wasn't sure if basketball was in my future.

My guidance counselor was also the boy's basketball coach, and in one of our meetings I told him about my hopes for college recruitment. He knew I was a standout on the team but he was realistic.

"Getting a scholarship to play ball in college isn't easy," he said. "But because your grades are so high there are a lot of academic scholarships you are eligible for, particularly ones for minorities."

"I don't qualify for those," I said.

He was silent for a moment, and then the conversation moved on.

My dad picked me up after practice that day, and I told him about our conversation.

He shook his head.

"But if people really think I qualify for them . . ." I ventured.

"It's dishonest," he replied without a moment's thought. "You'd be taking an opportunity away from someone who really needs it." Then he paused as if thinking something over and said, "Don't tell your mother about this."

I wondered how my dad could not notice that others assumed I was black. Once when we were in line to register for a basketball camp, the staff organizer cut the line off between my father and me. He assumed I was the child of the black woman standing in front of me, and not with the white man standing behind. I knew other people's perceptions were false, but it didn't change the facts of my experience. I got the message, though: I was not to even consider the possibility of identifying as black, and my family didn't want to talk about it.

I applied to Ivy League and liberal arts schools on the East Coast. I also applied to a few safety schools, including Carnegie Mellon University in Pittsburgh. I didn't want to stay in the 'burgh, as we called it, but CMU had a great reputation and was one of the only schools that continued to recruit me for their women's basketball team.

That spring, I went on an overnight visit to campus and stayed with the captain of the women's basketball team, Penny. She and the coach showed me around the gym, the weight room, and locker room. They described the travel schedule and that we'd fly to most away games. Then Penny took me to have dinner with her friends in their dorm. I'd never been in a dorm room, and the idea of living without parental oversight thrilled me. We stayed up late; I could hardly keep my eyes open, but I powered through because I didn't want to seem like a baby around the college seniors. They were four years older than I was, already in their twenties, drinking beer and cooking mac and cheese on their own hot plate! Their life was the stuff of fantasy.

When we woke up in the morning, Penny poured us bowls of cornflakes—and sprinkled chocolate chips in them. I couldn't believe what was happening; my parents would have never let me eat that for breakfast. I ate the cornflakes, still slightly crispy in the milk, with the bittersweet crunch of chocolate chips, and they tasted like freedom. I decided then and there that if I got in, I would go to Carnegie Mellon.

When we received the polite rejection letter from Princeton, my mom was heartbroken.

"That's where you should be," she said. I had gotten as far as the alumni interview, and my mom made tea and homemade biscotti for the man who came to interview me. We sat at the table in the kitchen, and when he asked me my plans, I told him I wanted to major in English and be a writer. The interview went well, I thought, and when he left, my parents were hopeful.

I didn't really care. My parents had driven us to New Jersey to visit Princeton, and the campus was beautiful. But I didn't get butterflies like I did when I ate those chocolate chips. The same was true when we flew to Cambridge to visit Boston College and Harvard. Tara came with us, and even when she ordered couscous at the restaurant—an unknown delicacy that we pronounced *cautious*—it did not stir my imagination the way the hot plate of mac and cheese did on my overnight visit.

I was waitlisted or rejected from the other schools to which I applied. When I finally received an acceptance letter from Carnegie Mellon University, it seemed like the obvious choice. Because my grades were so high, the school offered me the President's Scholarship, which would cover half my tuition every year. Since the school didn't offer athletic scholarships, I would have to try out for the basketball team, but it was understood that if I showed up, I would make the cut.

Despite the rejections from more prestigious schools, and despite staying in Pittsburgh, I was ecstatic. Carnegie Mellon felt like the place I wanted to be. Tara was going to the University of Pittsburgh, and we were excited because the campuses of Pitt and CMU were right next to each other in the hip neighborhood of Oakland. We had ventured down to the "O" for its trays of fries and the Beehive for vintage films and coffee, which we could barely choke down. Oakland was the first place I tried soy milk (terrible) and Greek food (pretty good). Even though we would still be in Pittsburgh, it felt like a world away, and we were excited to explore it together.

When I told my mom the good news, she acted as if I had thrown my college applications in the trash and set them on fire.

"If you want to stay in Pittsburgh, you should just go to Hills College," she said.

My dad tried to defuse the situation.

"If you want to go to Yale, I can get you in," he said. He explained that someone he worked with was an alumnus and that he was certain he could pull some strings.

I didn't want to go to Yale. Kyle Johnson was a senior on the boys' basketball team who wore his pants low, his hat backward, and went around spouting Public Enemy lyrics—the explicit versions. When he got into Yale he suddenly cleaned up his act, exchanging his rapper look for khakis and polo shirts. I thought Kyle Johnson was a poser, and his behavior made me suspicious about what it meant to attend an Ivy League school.

In addition to not wanting to be a poser, it seemed wrong that my dad would even suggest pulling some strings to get me into the Ivy League. Was our situation that desperate? Did he think the consolation prize of my attending Yale would really console my mom? I didn't want to get into college by the back door. My parents taught me not to take shortcuts, that I had to work harder than others to be rewarded. How was my dad asking a coworker to get me into Yale more honest than my applying for a minority scholarship? Wouldn't I be taking a spot away from someone who really wanted to be there?

When it came time for parent orientation at Carnegie Mellon, my mom refused to go. When my dad finally convinced her, she sat with her arms crossed and refused to wear the CMU PARENT button. Going to college was exciting, bewildering, and freeing, but a part of me internalized a sense of failure that came with my mother's disappointment. When we arrived on campus, my parents helped me carry all the new stuff they'd gotten me to my tiny room in Morewood Gardens. Even though my mom wished she were helping me settle in to a dorm at Princeton and despite her protestations, I knew she was proud of me. Like the day she dropped me off at the bus stop for my first day of school, I couldn't wait for what lay ahead, and she fought back tears as I waved goodbye.

Seven

My freshman year, I met Dave Jefferson, a football player in my World History class. The class was boring; a stout man with a gray beard and tweed jacket lectured to us on *Guns, Sails, and Empire*. Dave sat next to me and made jokes the whole time, raising his hand and giving absurd answers, which the professor mostly ignored. Dave had a raspy voice, a gap in his teeth, and a birthmark under his right eye. He was African American. He was kind of chubby, and I thought he was annoying but also kind of cute.

We began to talk outside of class, he mostly following me around campus, trying to make me laugh. His persistence paid off, and I started to see his personality—smart, charismatic, ambitious, quick-witted, but also attention-seeking and risk-taking. We began dating. We were both underage, but there was a bar near campus that always served him, and they served me as well. I liked that he seemed to have a pull with people, and I felt like a VIP when I was with him. One night, we stayed up all night in his apartment, talking. I finally fell asleep, and when I woke up on the couch, there was a single red rose next to me.

That morning, I had sex with Dave for the first time. Afterward, I sat in the bathroom, wondering if I felt different. Growing up in the Catholic Church, my teachers and parents made sex seem like a big deal. It was a sin unless you were married. Any person, especially a girl, who wanted to be good and moral should remain abstinent until marriage. My parents, who I knew conceived me before they were married, told me their situation was different; they were in love, and our family was destined from the start. My mother told me she had never been with anyone until she met my father. In high school, when she was a junior, she'd dated the captain of the basketball team, someone she'd had a crush on for years. But she waited and didn't give into temptation. Until she met my dad, she remained a virgin. We never talked about my dad's history, but it was implied that he had never been with anyone but my mother, even if that wasn't true. Their love for each other and me, the fact that they got married before I was born, and the fact that they told us our family was destined to be meant they could bend the rules a little. But the rest of us, especially good Catholic girls like me, should remain pure.

Still, before I went off to college, my mom took me to the doctor and told her to give me a prescription for birth control. I was offended. I was still a virgin, and my mom knew it. I was serious about my studies and about playing basketball; I had no intention of having sex in college. She explained to the doctor and me that it was to regulate my periods. As an athlete, my periods were irregular; this was true. But when my mom left the room, I voiced my concerns to the doctor. I wondered if knowing I was on the pill would lead me to do something I wasn't ready for. She replied, "You'll make the right decision."

When I lost my virginity with Dave, I was already on the Pill, and he used protection. I knew my mother became pregnant when she was nineteen, but at the moment, I wasn't worried about that. I thought about the girls in high school we knew who had sex and how my friends and I judged them as sluts. As I sat in the bathroom in Dave's apartment, I took a mental inventory of my body; everything felt normal. I'd heard you bled after having sex for the first time, but I didn't. It wasn't traumatic or life changing. I didn't feel like a different person. I realized sex wasn't as big a deal as everyone, including myself, made it out to be.

When Dave introduced me to his friends, his friend James, who was also black, asked me point-blank, "Are you black?"

"No," I said.

"Well, you're the blackest white girl I've ever seen."

When Dave took me to visit his family in Cincinnati, we stayed with his mother and grandmother. They were warm and welcoming. When we were in the car on the way to his dad's place, he leaned over and said, "Don't tell him you're white."

I introduced Dave to my parents, and they were kind and welcoming to him. My mom didn't protest, maybe because my relationship was happening while I was at college and not under her roof. Maybe she wasn't worried that I would get pregnant as long as I was on the Pill. When we talked, she never asked about Dave or my social life at school. She wanted to make sure I had enough food, clothes, and money, that I got the care packages she sent, and that I was keeping up with my studies.

Dave didn't seem to mind that I identified as white. He also didn't seem to mind when one of my friends from Russian class called me her "ghetto pass." I never mentioned my race to his father, or to his mother for that matter. Around his family I felt like I was passing as black. Dave knew my parents were white and he never confronted me about my racial identity. He never asked if I was adopted or mixed. Except for that moment in the car, my race was never an issue. We dated for almost two years until we had a messy breakup that ended with books flying and me chasing him out of my apartment with a frying pan.

I had quit the basketball team by then because I decided to major in Russian studies and knew that my basketball season, which took place during the winter, would conflict with the study-abroad program.

Carnegie Mellon wasn't a school known for its sports. The workouts and practices were grueling, but hardly anyone came to our games, and we didn't have a winning record. Playing basketball didn't give me the same celebrity it had in high school. It was a lot of work without any payoff, and I realized my heart was no longer in it. I went to see the coach with a lump in my throat, knowing that quitting went against the values my parents taught me. The longer I was away from home, though, the more I questioned those values. I knew I wasn't giving up; I was deciding to pursue a new passion and new opportunities. I knew my parents and coach would be disappointed, but my drive to study in Moscow overrode my fear.

My interest in Russia was piqued by a history course I'd taken as a senior in high school. The dramatic rise and fall of the tsars, the Russian Revolution, Lenin, Trotsky, and the Bolsheviks—it was a history that came alive for me, not like the stale triumphs of the Founding Fathers and the Revolutionary War that had been drilled into my head since elementary school. I never saw myself in American history, but for some reason Russian literature and history struck a chord. Dostoevsky, Tolstoy, Chekhov, and Gogol were writers who fought against the odds, writing against injustice, poverty, and censorship. I read about male and female characters wrestling with life's big questions and persevering when the world didn't make sense.

Amid brutality, these writers saw beauty; amid absurdity, meaning. Asking questions was more important than finding answers, and searching for the truth—even when the truth was ugly—was its own reward. Books like *Anna Karenina* and *Poor Liza* trod the worn ground of female protagonists annihilated by their own desires, but I found more that was familiar in these foreign worlds than I even had in the places I called home. The Russian language seemed laden with secret knowledge, and I wanted to unravel its mysteries. It was difficult, and I wanted the challenge. It was exotic, and I wanted to escape the mundane. Russia was foreign but not as inconceivable to me as the world of World Cultures had been in high school. In the end, my parents weren't upset that I chose my studies over basketball, but they were concerned that I'd decided to major in Russian with a secondary major in writing poetry.

"Can you get a job in that?" my mom asked. "Are you sure you don't want to go into medicine?"

I knew my parents would support me no matter what, and I promised myself that I would become the best writer and Russianist I could to prove I was worthy of that support.

Eight

In December 1998, I turned twenty. Two and a half years at college made me feel like a different person. I thought differently, spoke differently, and fancied myself one of the great minds of my time.

It was snowing in Pittsburgh, and the lampposts in Oakland were strung with wreaths and lights. In a few weeks, I would board a plane to Moscow, Russia. I was excited and nervous, eager to spend time with my friends over Christmas break before heading off into the unknown.

There was another unknown I was approaching, one much closer to home. I never talked to my friends seriously about my identity or race; I didn't have the language to talk about those things in a personal way, and more important, I was afraid to. But after two years of reading Heidegger and Dostoevsky I knew how to talk philosophy, and that is what I did.

As Tara and I drove the twenty miles north from Pittsburgh to the North Hills, the city gave way to gray rolling hills and bare-branched trees. A familiar malaise came over us.

"What are we going to do?" Tara said as we pulled into her

parents' driveway. "Spend another night at Denny's? It's the pit of despair, the trough of mediocrity. We have to be past that now. We're in college."

"You're right," I said. "The mind that strives toward higher realization is stifled there at the very gates. But we're not old enough to drink."

"So what, go to King's?"

King's wasn't open twenty-four hours on weeknights, so when the doors closed around eleven, we would hang out in the darkened parking lot, sitting on the curb by the dumpsters or squatting on the asphalt between our cars. As we slid into the rust-colored booth, a waitress served us coffee in the puffy-sleeved blouse and teal apron I'd worn just a few years before. It felt surreal. In high school, my privilege of driving the old blue Buick station wagon was passed to my brother Pat when he became a freshman, so during the summer, I walked up the highway shoulder to King's, stepping around broken bottles and roadkill, hoping the cars speeding around the winding road stayed in their lane. One day at the end of my shift, Pat came to pick me up, and instead of finishing wrapping my share of silverware in paper napkins, and despite the manager's protests, I decided to leave. The next day, I went in and was informed I had been fired for insubordination.

Tara and I sat in the smoking section, not because we smoked but because it was open later than the dining room. Diane, the waitress who served us our coffee, was legendary. She had worked at King's for thirty years, had no teeth, and was famous for her dirty mouth ("I'm going to come in my pants!") and racist humor ("That man just asked for a intentional of water!"). The smoking section was closest to the door and included a counter with stools that mainly served truckers who were coming in off the road for a quick no-frills meal and a smoke.

You had to be fast to work in this section. No one wanted to hear the list of daily specials, and they didn't care what your name was. You couldn't take time writing orders down in your pad. Diane served her customers with a permanent frown and few pleasantries, but she was the only one who could keep up.

"Hi, girls. Back on break?" Diane asked as she poured our coffee, but she was gone, pulling orders from the window before we could answer.

The waitress working the next section over saw us and waved. Her name was Linda, but we called her Trailer Trash Barbie. She was also a veteran waitress, with thickly caked foundation that only accentuated the hard lines of her face. She ignored the King's rule banning excessive jewelry, and there were rumors as to how she got away with it. Her unbuttoned blouse exposed tanned décolleté. The fitted apron barely reached the bottom of her skirt, and beneath that she wore thick tan pantyhose, white socks, and black sneakers. Her section was where the truckers usually sat for coffee.

I used to work in the section across from the stainless steel island of the dessert bar, with ladles sticking out of bins that held the dozen or so toppings for King's famous sundaes. I loved topping the sundaes with whipped cream not from a can but from a gun that was attached to a jug under the counter, or laying a slab of cinnamon ice cream onto a piece of hot apple pie. But my section was near the entrance to the kitchen, and diners had too clear a view of waitresses slopping soup into cups from crusty tureens and draining the water out of premade bowls of iceberg lettuce salads, one hand braced over the lettuce like a sieve.

After we got our coffee, Tara and I started in on the same conversation we'd been having for the last two and a half years.

"A set of values is given to you," I said, placing my hands on the table for emphasis. "You don't know how they function, but you use them anyway to uphold your happiness."

"Until they crumble," Tara said, "and you realize they were never *your* values."

"And it wasn't your happiness they were upholding."

There was a pause.

"When you live in a town where everyone knows you, you can live there for a long time and not change."

"Fuck, dude!" I said, slapping the table.

Tara could tell there was something on my mind that I wasn't saying. She said, "So what about tomorrow? The concert?"

"Dude, I don't even like Barenaked Ladies."

"I know, but it's something to do. Tomorrow's Friday, and if we end up sitting in a booth like this again, it will be clear to me—and I hope to you, too—that there really is no hope for us."

"Suppose we go to the concert. What then? Will our lives be any different? What about the next day and the day after that?" I paused. "Plus, tickets are, like, thirty bucks."

"Dude, your dad will give you thirty bucks."

I looked at the fake cuckoo clock on the wall. "We have one hour until Courtney can meet us. What do you want to do until then?"

"We could go to Perkins."

We liked Perkins because it was cleaner than Denny's, Eat'n Park, and King's, and an outstanding number of items were included in the price of a single meal. *Items* was a system of value-to-price ratio that my friends and I worked out from a story Tara told us about an old aunt who would sit her down in the kitchen and say, stabbing her finger into her palm, "Coffee. Eggs. Scrambled. Toast. Rye. Buttered. With jelly. Home fries. Sausage. Four links."

She'd pause, light a cigarette, take a drag, then finish, "Dollar ninety-nine."

Seven items for $1.99 was a mere myth to us, and every time we'd compare the items in, say, a Grand Slam or Moons Over My Hammy, we would see Tara's aunt's face, counting with us, serious as the grave.

Perkins closed early, so we arranged to meet Courtney at the Giant.

The Giant Eagle, the grocery store where my dad had gotten cupcakes on Pat's eighth birthday, was now the Super Giant Eagle. Open twenty-four hours, it was the only place other than a parking lot or cemetery that we could hang out late on a weeknight. My friends and I spent many nights combing the fluorescent-lit aisles long after the regular customers had gone home. The cashiers were all high school students, so they didn't care if we loitered.

We found Courtney sitting in the patio furniture display in the wide center aisle between candy and plastic dinnerware. We joined her under the pink-, orange-, and blue-striped umbrella, which shaded us from the harsh lights. An open box of powdered doughnuts sat on the table in front of us, their crumbs spilling onto the glass top.

"It's so lame," said Courtney, leaning back in the patio chair so that it rocked slightly. She pulled on the drawstrings of her hoodie. "There is no one in this town except us capable of having an intelligent conversation. All of this"—she motioned with her empty Mountain Dew bottle—"breeds complacency. Vulgarity. And we're stuck in the middle of it."

"Yeah," said Tara, wiping doughnut crumbs off the corner of her mouth. "The only things worth contemplating are the higher spiritual manifestations of the human intellect. Our entire concept of existence is built around the fact that we are never going to die. That's what makes this kind of life possible. But no one wants to talk about it. They just fill their carts up and load their shit into their SUVs."

I got up from the table and came back with a bag of Oreos, which I opened and put next to the doughnuts. From around the corner came a couple of stoner kids in long sweatshirts and baggy pants. They giggled and fake-punched each other when they saw us but kept stuffing bags of chips and candy into their pockets. Behind us loomed a tower of inflated beach balls. The other patio sets in the aisle were empty. Around us gleamed black and silver grills.

"Of course, the mind is not immortal; it's transitory, but I know what you mean," I said. "When a thinking person grows up and comes to awareness, you can't help feeling like life is some kind of trap from which there is no escape. Why you've been randomly brought into it out of nonbeing against your will . . . and you try to find some meaning, some goal of existence, but nobody tells you."

Each of our manifestoes was a testament to our fears at confronting the real world for the first time. We were talking about privilege and shame, about growing up and not knowing what came next. And we were saying that we would be there for each other, no matter what.

It was nearly two by then, and we got up from our oasis, stiff from rocking, paid for our half-eaten snacks, and stepped out into the supermarket lights. In the parking lot, Courtney went to her car, and we stood with her for a moment before getting in our parents' cars and driving home.

"Are you coming out tomorrow night?" Tara asked her.

"Can't. Matt's coming over."

In the car, Tara rolled down the window, letting the night air rush in.

"Let's go," she said, squinting against the sudden cold. "Seriously, we can't spend another night at the Giant. It'll be fun." Then casually, "Besides, Riley and Craig are coming."

"Oh," I said. "Really? Craig's back?"

"Yeah," she said. "He's back from Boulder on break."

"Oh," I said. "Okay, then. Yeah, I can get thirty bucks from my dad."

The next night when Tara picked me up, Craig and Riley were already in the car. I had a disposable camera, but we took so many pictures on the way to the concert that it ran out of film before we even got out of the North Hills. Tara with her thrift-store scarf and short hair in the driver's seat, turning around mid-laugh, mid-gesture. A blurred portrait of Craig and Riley posing with a Big Gulp, both of them in leather jackets, Riley with his black hair, looking like a freckled Tom Cruise, and Craig—with his mischievous eyes and broad frame—looking like no one but himself.

"Dad, pass that Big Gulp!" Craig yelled from the back seat. Music was blasting, one of Tara's mixtapes. I was lying on Craig's lap and got squished when he leaned forward to take the giant cup from Riley.

"Mom," yelled Craig again, "do you have any cigarettes?"

"What kind of mother would let her son smoke!" said Tara from the driver's seat.

"What kind of father would hand his son a bottle of whiskey!" laughed Riley from the passenger's seat, unscrewing the cap from a bottle of Old Grand-Dad.

"If you want to smoke, you'll have to ask your uncle," Tara said.

"Spoon?"

"Shit, dude, you know I don't smoke," I said.

We were a family. Kevin Riley was called *Dad*. He was Irish, the middle child of six. He and his siblings had cell phones and pagers before the rest of us even knew what they were. The only one of us who knew about responsibility, he would forgo hanging out on the weekends to clean newly built houses with his dad. He bought a truck with his own money while the rest of us were driving our parents' old beaters. After my St. Patty's Day party, it was Riley who brought over the steam cleaner to get the puke out of the carpet before my parents woke up.

The nurturing Tara and Courtney were both called *Mom*. Craig was their wild son, and I was their uncle. For unknown reasons, Craig's nickname for me was *Spoon*.

"How do you do it, Riley?" Tara asked.

"What?"

"Stay here and not get freaked out! I feel like this place is eating me alive, but you said you're thinking of buying a house?"

"Yeah," said Riley. "So?"

"So—don't you even want to get away from your parents?"

"Well, I work with my dad."

"But how can you even stand them? Aren't you pissed at them for raising you here in the first place?"

"My parents moved up here so we could have a better life," Riley said.

"Jesus, Riley, you sound just like my father!" said Tara. "What's 'better' about being in the suburbs? My dad's a parole officer and used to take me to the city with him when he'd go check on his parolees. I got to see DeVon at his barbershop. That's where I used to get my hair cut! Those people have real lives and real trouble—"

"That's the point, Mom."

At the concert, we merged with the stream of bodies working its way up to the dark heights of the amphitheater. We spiraled up the concrete stairwell, grasping the sticky handrail, breathing the air humid with warmth and voices. The crush of bodies made my head spin. A few steps above me, Tara's rear was in my face. Craig was pushing me up the steps with his whole body.

Craig came to our high school a year before we graduated, a rare transfer from out of state. His parents moved a lot for business, although we never learned which. They moved from California, but we never learned where he was actually from. Tall, with sandy hair and an easy laugh, he'd put his arm around me when we were sitting in Riley's basement and I was getting into some heated philosophical debate. He'd say, "Why do you always have to be so deep, Spoon?" He worked out at 5:00 a.m. before school every day and played varsity football, but you wouldn't know it from his baggy T-shirts and go-with-the-flow attitude.

Once when his parents were away in South America, he called me at six in the morning. He told me that he and Riley had been up all night drinking, and Riley had just gone home.

When I got there, he went down to the basement and came up with an unmarked bottle.

"You have to try this, Spoon," he said. He got out two glasses and poured the golden liquid. He gave one to me, clinked glasses, and downed his in one gulp. I sniffed at mine and tentatively sipped. All of a sudden, I felt a wave of sweet sun, like I was transported to a carnival, laughing and twirling in the warm breeze.

"This could be our place," he said, putting his glass down and moving toward me.

"When are your parents getting back?" I asked.

"They were supposed to be back yesterday."

We were almost at the top of the amphitheater. "What do you want to do after this?" Craig said in my ear.

"I don't know," I said. "Tara and I were probably going to spend the night in Oakland."

"Maybe Mom can go home," he said.

"Mom's driving."

By the time we reached our seats, we were dripping sweat, dizzy with vertigo and liquor. My vision became kaleidoscopic as we filed into the long, horseshoe curve of our row. Thousands of waving bodies spun and fragmented into more thousands. We had to hold onto each other for support. The seats were bad, but it didn't matter.

"Here you go, Son," said Tara, fumbling around in her bag. She opened her backpack, took out a bottle of vodka, and handed it to Craig.

"Thanks, Mom," he said. He opened it and took a long swig. He passed it to me, but I shook my head.

"Pop!" he said, handing it to Riley.

"Thanks, Son," he said. He put his arm around Tara. "We sure are proud of our boy."

When the lights went down, the crowd's roar greeted the band onstage. In a sea of swaying lights, the band played "Hello City." They jumped around, improvised, switched instruments, but I felt as if I were on a different planet.

Craig's hand was resting against my leg.

"Maybe none of this, these people, this concert, really exists," I said to him. "Maybe we're dreaming them, and when we wake, we'll realize we're in some other time."

"Spoon!" he said.

"Don't you ever have the feeling that you aren't really you? That the face you see in the mirror, the eyes you're looking out of, is some-one or something else? Do you know what I mean?"

Craig took another swig of vodka. "I think you think too much, Spoon!" he said and laughed.

"I know you think about this, too!" I said. My eyes were closed, and I was slurring my speech. I was drunk. Craig laughed, and I let myself fall against him, laughing, too.

"Come back with me after," he said, brushing his lips against my neck.

Mother, Son, and Uncle went back to my place in Oakland after the show. Dad went home so he could get up early for a job.

I lived on the attic floor where the roof slanted nearly to the ground. My three roommates, two of them former basketball team-mates, were away for break with their own families.

The dark, empty house swayed around us as we climbed the stairs. Unopened mail covered countertops; the basement was filled with old bikes, philosophy books, broken furniture, and desk lamps aban-doned by students who'd lived there before. Metallic ferns crept along green wallpaper.

Tara watched Craig and me undress each other. My futon was rickety, and from the way Craig let himself fall against it, I knew he wouldn't last long. Soon Craig passed out, naked, in my bed. Tara went back to the cot in the adjoining room. I threw the covers over Craig and myself and went to sleep.

It was still early when we got back to Wexford. Craig was still groggy. Tara helped me dress him, load him into the car, and drive him home. We had to pull over a couple of times on the way back so he could open the car door and vomit.

After we dropped Craig off at his parents' house (they weren't home), Tara and I drove to Denny's.

We ordered coffee and began to flip through the sticky, plastic-coated menus.

"I can't stand this," said Tara. "I live in constant agonizing terror that the best ideas of my life are being sucked away." She took a sip of coffee and lowered her voice. "I dream I'm visited by messengers from the future. People come to me, whispering in a language I can't understand, giving me instructions, telling me to follow them—but I don't know how, and they vanish."

"We're all going to die," I said, wincing at the bitterness of my coffee. When I went to college, I stopped adding cream and sugar.

"I want to be cremated," Tara said. "My aunt was buried alive. They thought she was dead, had a funeral and everything. Someone walking through the graveyard heard a noise coming from one of the headstones. They dug her up and found her lying there, eyes wide open." Tara waved to the waitress for more coffee.

"Conflict, sensitivity to pain . . . ," I continued.

"Eggs. Scrambled. Coffee . . ." Tara was studying the menu.

"I mean, it's 1998—"

"With cream. Toast—"

"People say Chekhov wrote about despair—"

"Wheat. With butter."

"But he wrote!" I said, slapping the table.

"Bacon. Four pieces—"

"How is that despair?"

"French toast. Powdered sugar."

"And how do we know if that peace or despair is outside or within us? A hundred years later and we're still asking the same questions!"

"Three sixty-nine."

The booths were yellow, the carpet a horrible paisley. We hated the neckties worn by the waitstaff, with drawings of suns, houses, kids, and doggies made by children who were either in cancer hospitals or who were raising money to support children in cancer hospitals. We hated the smudged glass of the claw machine, the cheap stuffed animals inside, and the fact that nobody could ever win.

Just then, we saw Denise, the manager, a pale, flustered woman with a limp ponytail, going up to tables on the other side of the restaurant and escorting customers out the door. Even those mid-meal looked up, confused, and left their seats.

"See that?" Tara said. "You live your life in this cistern, and one day you crack. Look—she's totally lost it!"

I took another sip of coffee.

"Hey, I think something's going on—"

There was a loud crash in the kitchen, and that's when we saw it. The line cook yelled something to Denise, but he was soon obscured by billows of black smoke that poured out of the order window. We didn't wait for Denise, who was screaming by then. As we filed out the door, Tara noted that it would be a good time to break the glass and raid the pie case and the claw machine, but we didn't.

Once in the parking lot, we heard the pops and cracks of the roof buckling under the flames. Smoke filled the sky over Denny's like an evil cloud.

We got into the car and pulled into a used car dealership across the street to watch the scene. The roof had caved in by then, and flames shot freely into the sky. Smoke trickled out the windows and rose from the crack under the door. Sirens sounded in the distance and grew shrill as fire trucks came speeding up Route 19. Firefighters jumped from the truck, unwound the hose, and began to spray arcs of water into the flames.

We sat in silence for a few moments. The time for philosophizing was over. I was going to Moscow and one of our childhood hangouts was burning down before our eyes. I felt schadenfreude, triumph, and some other feelings I couldn't name.

Nine

My senior year in college, I stole a ring. It was a claddagh ring, cheap, not even real silver. My friends and I were at a St. Patrick's Day festival in Pittsburgh. Under the beer tents and strung lights, we browsed vendor booths, looking, hoping, for something magical to spring forth from the usual hoards of KISS ME I'M IRISH T-shirts, novelty flags, plastic hats, shamrocks, and costume jewelry. My friends went to get a beer, which I declined. One had already splashed down my leg when a drunken stranger knocked into me. My skin was sticky, my wet sandaled foot attracting gravel. Stale beer, a smell I hated, clung to me like sweat. I shrugged off the irritation as I browsed the display cases of jewelry while I waited on my friends.

Chunky veined turquoise, Celtic knots and crosses, and the familiar symbol of two hands holding a heart. In high school, my friends and I all had rings like that; it was a common token of Irish heritage. We wore the rings, called claddagh, upside down with the heart pointing toward our bodies to symbolize friendship and family loyalty.

The festival was loud, and the booth was busy with people coming and going. As my fingers slid down the surfaces of the rings, I felt how loosely they were held in the little slits of fake black velvet. The vendor's back was turned. Before I realized what I was doing, my finger slid one of the heart-shaped rings into the cuff of my sleeve and held it there. I browsed for a few more seconds and then went to find my friends.

I found them in front of a stage where a folk band was getting ready to play. The ring was in my pocket, and I was nervous. Maybe it was my foul mood after having a beer spilled on me, maybe it was the feeling that this debauchery was no way to celebrate Irish heritage.

On St. Patrick's Day, my mother always made Irish soda bread and lamb stew. My grandfather taught us the Wolfe Tones' version of "My Heart Is in Ireland" and bought us CDs of the Clancy Brothers and Tommy Makem, wearing their cream-colored Aran sweaters. Every member of my family had one of those sweaters. I had a turtleneck version, with a thick rolled collar and long cuffed sleeves. As I stood in the crowd, I could still remember the smell of the wool, wet with melted snow, as I peeled my coat off in the kitchen on a snow day.

That evening, I was wearing a red minidress and a light jacket. I was conscious of my bare legs because of the beer and because I didn't usually wear short skirts. With the ring in my pocket, my nervousness became paranoia, and I wished the droning band would stop. I looked around. Had somebody seen me take the ring? Would they confront me?

I was self-conscious because of something else, too. That night when I told my friends I was Irish, they responded, "Yeah! Everyone's Irish on St. Patrick's Day!" and raised their glasses in a cheer. That wasn't what I meant, I thought. I knew my classmates saw me as somehow "ethnic," but I still felt connected to a sense of identity

I got from my parents, how we defined ourselves and our culture as a family. In my heart, I knew there was a difference between us, one I was terrified to confront. I felt a pang that night with my friends, and it didn't take me long to notice that no one in the crowd was "Irish" like I was.

Mercifully, the music ended, and we shuffled along with everyone else to the exit. The crowd made our bodies invisible, and with a slight movement of my hand, I reached into my pocket, palmed the stolen ring, and dropped it into the dust. *Good*, I thought. I had corrected my strange, criminal act before anything happened. I had brought balance back to my universe. The ring was gone now. My conscience should have been clear—but it wasn't.

Before we could exit the fairground, a security guard stopped us. He was standing with the vendor from the booth where I'd found the ring. He looked me up and down and told me the vendor said I'd stolen something from the booth. Blood rose to my cheeks, adrenaline surged, and my chest tightened. I acted indignant, enraged. I told him I had no idea what he was talking about. I turned out my pockets, revealing only lint. I didn't dare look the vendor in the eye. The guard nodded and reluctantly let us pass.

My friends stayed silent through the whole scene. I was alone at the booth, so they didn't know whether anything had happened or not. When we got to the parking lot, one of them broke the silence.

"I can't believe they did that," she said. "Just because you're the only—" She stopped, not knowing how to say what I was out loud. I said nothing. I liked that she was indignant on my behalf. I liked that she assumed I was innocent and had been singled out because I was different. I didn't want to think about how things would have gone if I hadn't unloaded the ring in time. I didn't even know why I'd taken it in the first place.

As we drove back to campus, the conversation shifted to other things, but I was still raw and shaking from the confrontation. I felt transparent and vulnerable, like I'd been found out, like the guard knew exactly who and what I was and—unlike my friend—would not have been afraid to say it. In the glare of those lights, I let my silence cast me as the victim, my friend's defense wrapped around me like a warm but itchy sweater. The telltale ring was gone, ground down like a beer tab, a scrap of no consequence. But tears burned in the back of my throat, and all the way home, I wanted to confess.

I wrote about the incident in my poetry class. Like always, my professor, Jim Daniels, gave detailed feedback, filling the margins with check marks and suggestions. The semester was almost over, and I had already decided to apply to doctoral programs in Russian literature instead of MFA programs for writing. I went to Jim's office to ask him about writing opportunities outside of graduate school.

"I liked the poem you wrote for class," he said. "There's a summer workshop for African American poets I think you should attend. It's called Cave Canem."

I demurred. I wasn't sure this was for me, even after my experience at the St. Patrick's Day festival, even after all the experiences throughout my life that told me in whispers and shouts that I was not who I thought I was. I thought about my family and how, in their eyes, my identifying as anything but Irish and Italian was dishonest.

I looked up to Jim. He showed me what it was like to be a poet in real life. He was a regular person; he had a family. He invited students over to his house for a barbecue at the end of the year, and we played four square with his kids in the backyard. He showed me you didn't have to be a crazy drug addict or some cliché from a Jack Kerouac novel to be an amazing writer. His example made me feel validated. If I wanted to be a writer, I didn't have to be anything other than who I was. But that was the problem; as I sat in his office, I wasn't sure.

"Toi Derricotte runs the workshop," Jim continued after I failed to give him a response. "She teaches over at Pitt." He pulled a slim book down from his shelf. "You should read this," he said.

I took the book in my hands. It had a red cover with a small house made out of black bars in the center. At the bottom was the author's name, and at the top was a single word: *Captivity*.

"Okay," I said and got ready to leave the office. "Thanks."

"Let me know what you think," he said and added before I walked out the door, "No matter what else you're doing, just keep writing."

In my attic room, I devoured the book. I was struck by a poem about the author as a little girl being dragged by her grandmother through Saks Fifth Avenue. The little girl is tired, her legs ready to give out, but her light-skinned grandmother won't risk causing a scene because she and her granddaughter are passing for white. The grandmother basks in the deference of the salesclerks as they help the little girl try on velvet stockings; she knows what it's like to walk on thin ice and wants to instill in the girl that when she is in public, she can never, ever let her guard down. When the girl's legs finally give out, her grandmother pulls her up by the hair and rushes out of the building, away from eyes she fears see past her fancy clothes and light skin, down to genes that give her away.

I thought about the time I went to Saks Fifth Avenue with my mother to shop for a prom dress. The saleswomen were obliging and cooed over me as I tried on expensive dresses. I was tall, fair, and slim, and they looked good on me. With my hair in a fluffy coif, I looked as if I'd curled it to give it volume, not straightened it to hide its natural kink. We purchased a tastefully fitted black dress with a black sequined bodice and left the store without incident.

At school functions, my mother would whisper to me to comb my hair if she thought it looked too frizzy; when we went out together, I knew to slick it back into a tight ponytail or at least pull the front back, away from my face.

Even though it was easier for me to wear my hair in its "wild" state, I knew that for any special occasion I needed to fix it. The fanciest way to fix my hair, I learned, was to straighten it, and my mom was happy to oblige.

The first method she tried was laying my head down on the ironing board and running the hot, steaming iron over my hair.

"This is how we did it when I was in high school," she said.

It may have worked in the '70s, for my mom and her friends, whose hair was almost straight to begin with, but it burned my scalp and singed the brittle ends of my hair. I went to bed that night smelling like burned toast.

A more successful method involved using a blow dryer and brush. The result was a puffy cloud rather than straight tresses, but it was as close as we could get. We never thought of using a flatiron or lye relaxer on my hair, as those products were meant for black women.

Straightening my hair as well as we could and curling it with a curling iron became the norm for special occasions like my prom and senior photos. I wondered about the hair of the girl in the poem: Was it straight, curled, wavy, or pulled back into neat, tight pigtails? I thought about her grandmother's pride and paranoia. Did my mother feel like that when we went out? Was her insistence on my combing my hair, which by the way would never tame its frizz, her way of making sure, at least in her mind, that I could pass?

She said my hair should always look neat, and I admired the white girls in my school whose curly hair fell in smooth ringlets around their faces. *Why can't mine look like that?* I thought.

The girl in the poem seemed reluctant to go along with her grandmother's charade, but I threw myself into the role of the well-groomed, well-behaved daughter. I wanted my parents' praise and the praise of other adults; if that meant having straight hair, acting ladylike, and not rocking the boat in any way, I was willing to do it.

But now I felt split in two: Was I the stone-faced grandmother soldiering on, dragging her granddaughter by the hair along with her, or the little girl who just wanted to be herself? I felt like both. The little girl in me was tired; my emotional legs were about to collapse. A will stronger than my own held me upright, but I knew it could not last much longer.

Ten

I found out that I had been admitted to grad school in April 2001, while I was working as a food runner at the White Dog Café in Philadelphia.

The work of grad school was overwhelming. Each day I lived in fear that I would never finish all the work I had to do, and each day I came to class having read, written, and prepared more than I thought possible. Much of our work was in Russian, and many of my fellow graduate students were native speakers of Russian or another Slavic language. It took me four years of college, one semester of study abroad in Moscow, one intensive summer language program at Middlebury College, and one summer as a Rotary volunteer in Kamchatka to gain not only native fluency in Russian, but also the ability to closely read, analyze, and write critically about Russian literature. While still an undergraduate I wrote and presented conference papers in Russian, translated Russian poetry, and guest taught an advanced Russian language class. I passed Princeton's oral entrance exam with the department's preeminent professor of Soviet literature, himself a native of the former Soviet Union. I dreamed in Russian. I lived in

Vienna, Austria, for three months to study German to gain the additional fluency required for admission. I was one of only two students admitted to Princeton's Slavic program that year, and yet, as my time in the program went on, my terror intensified and I felt like an imposter.

My classmates felt that way, too. Each of us was a kind of Russian literature superhero, but our professors remained unimpressed with our daily feats of linguistic expertise and encyclopedic scholarship. We soon learned that our extraordinary efforts were nothing special. We did earn praise now and then—perhaps on a particularly prescient passage in an essay. In the seemingly endless desert of harsh appraisal, those moments were precious drops of water to slake our thirst for validation. Fear of repudiation overrode our desire to participate, and during our seminars, even when we knew the answers to our professors' questions, we sat in subdued silence.

Eleven

During my graduate program, I took every opportunity I could to write. Tara was in film school in New York City, and we took the train to visit each other, exchanged stories and mused about becoming writers.

In the fall of my fifth year, I took an undergraduate poetry workshop. The course was taught by the awe-inspiring Yusef Komunyakaa. The class met in his office, and most days we went around the room commenting on each other's poems. One day, a girl spoke up about a poem I'd written about Whole Foods.

"I don't like the fact that the boy pushing carts has cornrows," she said. Komunyakaa said nothing, but we shared a look. The student went on, "I mean, I know that's probably how it was, and there's nothing wrong with it, but I don't know. I just don't like it."

I had no response, and eventually the discussion moved on. But something had happened. I'd recognized it, and Komunyakaa had, too. We shared a moment of recognition.

When the year was about to end, just as I had done as a senior in college, I headed to my poetry professor's office to ask him about writing opportunities I could pursue. There was something else I wanted to ask him, too, but I didn't know if I'd have the courage.

Reds and oranges spread against an overcast New Jersey sky as I crossed the parking lot and opened the door to 185 Nassau Street, the university's arts building. I was nervous as I walked down the echoing hallway, passing faculty offices with names like Paul Muldoon and Joyce Carol Oates on the doors. The floor was polished white, reflecting the lights overhead. I'd read that 185 Nassau Street once housed the city of Princeton's first integrated elementary school. I wondered how the university fit into that legacy, whether the school's founders would have marveled or shuddered at the building's future.

I'd opened Yusef Komunyakaa's door dozens of times on my way to poetry class, but today I was opening a door to something else altogether. It was every door I'd stood before my entire life when I had the chance to confront my racial identity but was afraid to. It was the door I'd stood before in high school when I considered applying to minority scholarships for college. It was the door I'd stood before as a sixth grader when a doctor waited for my mother to leave the exam room and then asked me if I was black. It was the door I'd stood before as an undergrad when Jim Daniels suggested I apply to the Cave Canem poetry workshop and I turned the opportunity down. I felt the old conflict between loyalty to my family and loyalty to myself. I didn't want to be dishonest, and my desire to know the truth about myself was fraught with guilt. Now I felt as though I couldn't keep that door closed any longer.

I looked up to Yusef Komunyakaa the same way I looked up to Jim Daniels. I didn't want my writing to disappoint him, but more than that, *I* didn't want to disappoint.

When Jim told me about Cave Canem and asked me if I'd considered attending, it was easy for me to say no. I didn't realize it then, but in one crucial way, Jim had been like every other teacher, guidance counselor, and coach that had ever advised me to take an opportunity meant for minorities: he was white. Without my realizing it, their whiteness acted as a kind of buffer for me. White people had been asking me questions about my identity my whole life, and ultimately they accepted whatever answer I gave them. Maybe they thought I was lying or trying to pass. Maybe they could see that my denial was the result of a family secret and decided not to get involved. But no matter how unsatisfying my answers were to them, no one ever pushed the issue. Even though I was constantly questioned about my hair, family, and *nationality*—the euphemism used for *ethnicity* or *race*—no one took it very far. Without realizing it, I had always taken comfort in the white gaze that didn't want to peer too deeply into the chasm of race and discover what, if anything, it had to do with them.

Growing up, I had few black people in my life: my first boyfriend in college, some friends in high school and middle school, and an assistant high school basketball coach. I was friends with my coach and admired her, but we never talked about my race. So I wasn't ready for the feeling I had when I encountered a black mentor to whom I felt accountable for hiding behind my whiteness.

Now I felt vulnerable and exposed, but not in the same way I had at the St. Patrick's Day festival. I didn't feel like I would be punished for what the looker saw. The feeling was at once a relief and a journey into uncharted waters. I had no map for these feelings or what this kind of recognition meant. I squirmed under the newness of the black gaze.

Komunyakaa's door was slightly ajar. I knocked, my hand barely touching the door, and it opened. As I entered, I could feel his languid gaze, his ever-present half smile.

We sat in silence for a moment or two, him waiting patiently, me having no idea how to express all the feelings and questions welling up inside me.

"I think you have a question for me," he said in his deep Louisiana drawl. He looked me right in the eye.

The directness of his statement caught me off guard. I had planned to mention, casually, that I'd been reading his poem "Ode to the Drum" and that I'd learned to make a goatskin drum at a pottery workshop I'd attended before grad school. This now seemed incredibly stupid, nothing more than a student trying to impress her teacher. I sat there for what felt like too long without saying anything, without asking the question that he knew I had come to ask.

After fifteen minutes or so of chatting about the Polish editions of his work and his dislike of performance poetry, I managed to get around to my main questions: How should I continue writing? What opportunities are out there for me? I couldn't take another undergraduate class, and I could not imagine finishing a Ph.D. and then enrolling in an MFA program. Did he have any suggestions?

They were simple enough questions, but in them was everything I'd been avoiding for the last five years—indeed, for my whole life. My eyes welled with tears, and I clenched my jaw to keep it from shaking.

If he noticed, he didn't let on.

"Well, there's the *Callaloo Creative Writing Workshop*. That's good because it's two weeks. Have you heard of it?" He said this very casually as if it were the most normal conversation in the world. To anyone other than me, it would have been.

"No," I managed.

"It's for African diaspora poets and fiction writers. The deadline hasn't passed yet. You can still apply for this summer."

"Okay, thanks," I said.

There was so much more I wanted to say, to ask. I wanted his blessing, his validation. I wanted him to tell me there was nothing wrong with the life I'd lived up to this point, the life my parents chose for me and that I'd consented to in order to please them and make things easier for myself. I wanted him to tell me that none of it was my fault; that I was just being a good, loyal daughter who had no reason to suspect her parents would lie about something so fundamental.

I wanted him to tell me I wasn't a traitor or a coward, but as I left his office, those were the only two words screaming over and over in my head.

Whether I realized it or not, in his own way, he had given me what I wanted.

As I left the arts building and walked out into the fall day, I felt like I had been beaten to a thin skin and stretched to the point of tearing apart. I was neither a gazelle nor a panther, but all the secrets that had been trapped inside my old body now resonated from me in a new sound—beautiful, foreign, and terrifying.

It was windy and dark when I got home from campus. Wind rattled the doors and windows of the small house I shared with Fang Fang, a doctoral student in aerospace engineering. I closed the front door as quietly as I could and tiptoed across the linoleum floor so as not to disturb my housemate. Was she home? Even though the doors and walls were thin, I hardly ever heard her moving around the house. Her bedroom door was always closed, and I never dared knock.

I needed to unload my books and gather some things to take to my friend Sveta's house. We were in the final stages of planning a graduate student conference. It was hard to shift my mind from my inner turmoil to the task of scheduling panels, printing posters, and making arrangements for guests, but it was also a welcome distraction.

Before I left my room, I sat down at my desk and opened my laptop. My meeting with Komunyakaa was all I could think about. The most important question was: What happens next? Just as when I was an undergraduate, I knew there were other workshops I could attend, other scholarships for which I could apply. There were workshops for women, emerging writers, experienced writers, young writers, older writers, poets, fiction writers, regional writers, and international writers. I didn't think that workshops or grants for African Americans were the only ones out there. The issue was about finding support in a community. I was tired of existing in what felt like a vacuum of racial ambiguity. Since I grew up identifying as white, I knew the social codes. I knew how to affirm my belonging in mostly white groups, which often included subtly disparaging other races. Those moments became increasingly uncomfortable. I was tired of playing along; the more aware I became of others questioning my identity the more isolated I felt. I felt adrift on a sea of contradictions that would not resolve until it was I, not others, who defined who I was. For that to happen, I needed to know for certain on which side of the color line I stood, and there was only one person who could answer that question.

I opened my email, clicked Compose, typed in my mother's email address, and let the cursor blink in an empty field. I knew the gist of the email I needed to write but didn't know how to phrase it. With a few simple words, I could open a Pandora's box that my family had kept carefully closed for twenty-seven years.

I knew my mother was my biological mother. The words *Who is my father?* were straightforward enough, but they were loaded with the emotional and psychological freight of a lifetime. My Irish American father had raised me since I was in my mother's womb. They married when she was twenty and he was twenty-one because she was pregnant with his child, or so they believed.

So what happened?

Who was the person who intervened in my family's history, and who was he to my mom?

Why had she married my father and not him?

Could I find and get to know this person now?

Did I even want to?

These questions were the reason my ethnicity was taboo in our family. If I were black, then I had a different father, and my mother had been with another man. I'd never been able to consider that possibility, and perhaps, for her own reasons, neither could my mother.

I let the cursor blink. It was too much to handle at that moment. I didn't know how to phrase my questions, and I wanted to ask them gently. The thing I feared most, even more than what would happen to my world if I found out the truth, was that even asking would hurt my mother. What compelled her to ignore and avoid the question for twenty-seven years?

Twelve

"Hey, Sveta, Martin," I said, shaking my jacket off in the doorway, nodding to my friend and her husband. When I got into the apartment, I could hear their upstairs neighbor practicing chords on his bass.

"He's figured out it sounds better if he leaves out the fourth and seventh on the runs," Martin said, closing the door behind me. Martin had a nasal voice and a penchant for pointing out facts that no one asked for. I wasn't as good of friends with Martin as I was with Sveta, who was one of the first people I'd met in my program, but they were a package deal. Anything you wanted to tell one you had to tell the other.

I was all set to tell them about my meeting with Yusef Komun-yakaa and my decision to email my mom about the question of my race, but when I looked at Sveta, I noticed that she was even paler than usual with dark purple rings under her eyes. Sveta was eight months pregnant and a workaholic like the rest of us, organizing the graduate conference, going to prenatal yoga and therapy twice a week, and working on her dissertation.

"Are you okay?" I asked as I joined Sveta on the couch. I expected her to give me some graphic description of the symptoms she was experiencing from her pregnancy, which she had done before; whether it was her Slavic forthrightness, her personality, or both, she had no filter when it came to delivering sensitive information.

"It's Angie," she said, unscrewing the top from her blue Nalgene bottle with a slim-wristed hand. "Something happened; she told me not to go into any details . . ."

I waited, watching the deliberation play out of Sveta's face. Angie had graduated three years ago and moved to Texas with her husband, Ryan, but things hadn't gone well.

"Ryan wants a divorce," Sveta revealed, not able to hold back. "Angie thinks he's cheating on her."

"Jesus," I said.

"There's something else, too," Sveta continued. "She kind of prostituted herself for crack."

"What?" I didn't think I'd heard her right. I knew Angie liked to get drunk at parties—we all did—but I had no idea she would do something like that.

"She didn't mean to," Sveta continued. "And she didn't have sex with anyone. She was at a motel, and these guys asked her if she wanted to party, and things just got out of hand. She's won't talk to her therapist about it and is threatening to commit suicide."

"A black guy gave her the crack in his car," Martin chimed in from his seat at the computer. "But he made her watch him masturbate first."

It sounded more like sexual assault than prostitution. I couldn't imagine what Angie must have been going through, how scared and vulnerable she must have felt—and how desperate.

Angie was fluent in a dozen languages instead of only three or four like the rest of us. She wrote her private journal in Czech and was fluent in American and Spanish sign language. In addition to feeling bad for Angie, I didn't understand how she could feel so bad about herself that she'd let herself get into such a situation. I didn't know how she could have felt so alone. Didn't she know she was worth more than that, that there were people who loved her and would listen to whatever troubles she had? Didn't she know that her life meant something to us? To me?

I didn't know what to make of Martin specifying that the man who took advantage of her was black. Was it necessary to tell us that? Did it make her already terrifying experience even scarier or more dangerous? Is that what Angie conveyed when she'd told Sveta the story? Martin didn't mention the race or ethnicity of the other guys at the party.

"I told her to come here and stay with us," Sveta said. "David's going to be in town, too, and she could use the moral support."

David had graduated two years before and was now an assistant master at one of the residential colleges at Harvard.

"That's a good idea," I said, "but are you sure you're up to it? You look pretty worn out."

Sveta had been keeping Angie on the phone all night to make sure she didn't harm herself. It was obvious she'd lost a couple of nights' sleep, and being so far along in her pregnancy, that could be dangerous.

"Why doesn't she stay with me?" I volunteered. "I'm sure my housemate won't mind."

"Didn't you say you had something you wanted to talk about?" Sveta asked me, remembering why I'd come over. "You sounded kind of worried on the phone." She stretched out her arm with the now empty water bottle, and Martin rose to fill it.

"No," I said. "It's not a big deal. It can wait."

We got down to making final plans for the conference, but even as I double-checked the housing arrangements and worried about our friend, my mind kept creeping back to what I had experienced that day. I desperately wanted to tell my friends about my own emotional turmoil, but how could I dump my problems on them with everything else that was going on?

"Hold on," Sveta said, pushing herself up from the couch. "I have to pee. I pee about every fifteen minutes."

"The book says that's normal," Martin called from the kitchen.

"I'm going to get going," I said to Martin while Sveta was still in the bathroom. It felt a bit strange to announce this while Sveta was out of the room, and for a moment, Martin and I stood there looking at each other awkwardly.

"Well, then," he said, full water bottle in hand, "I'll tell her you had to go."

We made some small talk on the way to the door. I laughed at things he said that I didn't think were funny. It was a habit I'd started to notice recently—the friendly persona I often showed when all I really wanted was to close down into myself. Why did I need to expend so much energy to make others comfortable when I wasn't? It was something I'd always done, even when I was a kid: a quick joke, a smile, even laughter. Lots of nodding and facial expressions that showed I was listening.

Most of the time, I didn't even notice that I put on this type of show, but lately the forced extroversion made me feel depleted. It wasn't only discomfort I was masking. At some point in my childhood, I must have learned that a girl, especially one whose difference was noticeable to those around her, should always smile and be polite and cheerful to put others at ease. I was eager to please my parents, coaches, and teachers. I couldn't stand the feeling that I might let someone down who had put their faith in me. But I was equally eager to placate acquaintances and strangers. Was it just a habit, or did I feel like I had to constantly apologize for being who I was?

I was so eager to please that I even took on extra work. I was planning one conference with Sveta, but I also agreed to help out with another that wasn't my field, to fill in for someone who had backed out at the last minute. I remembered agreeing with enthusiasm, without a second thought, even though in truth, when I stopped to think about it, participating in a conference on Victorian English literature was the last thing I wanted to do. Who was I trying so hard to please?

This barrage of thoughts went through my mind in the moment it took for Martin to walk me to the door. As I stepped out into the chilly evening, I wondered where all these new realizations were coming from, and I wondered why I suddenly felt so angry.

Thirteen

When I got home, the rain was beating on our roof. I opened my email again and thought about how to broach the subjects of my ethnicity and paternity to my mother.

My dad always told us that in Ireland, *Dunn* meant "the dark clan." Almost everyone on his side of the family had dark hair, light eyes, and tanned rather than burned in the sun. He said his grandmother, who had black hair until she died, was part Native American. His mother was supposed to be German, but she looked like she could have been Spanish with her light olive skin and black hair. His brother, my uncle John, had dark curly hair, and when I was little, everyone said that my curly hair came from the same genes. Maybe the source of my dark features lay somewhere in my parents' genes, after all. They say characteristics can skip a generation or two. Maybe I was the perfect genetic blip.

Deep down, I knew this wasn't true, though as I approached the precipice of finding out for sure, part of me wanted it to be. Since the subject of my race had always been taboo in my family, it seemed important for them to see me as white, no matter what kind of explanations they had to invent. I worried that acknowledging I was black and had a different father from the one I grew up with could shatter the unity of the family my parents had worked so hard to create.

My rational mind knew I was not responsible for the way I'd been born and that I was entitled to know who my father was, but I felt guilty for stirring up what I knew would be a terrible family conflict. I felt guilty for my own denial and resentful of my parents for theirs.

Fourteen

Paper clips, spare change, glue, combination locks, tape measures, Scotch tape, masking tape, cassette tapes, rubber bands, pencils, address books, sticky notes, light bulbs, batteries, nails, screws, keys, twist ties, sequins, matches, thumbtacks—all of these and more floated in the tangled swamp of the junk drawer at our house on Lincoln Boulevard. Need a hammer? It might be in there, or it might be in there one day and gone the next. It created the eerie feeling of constantly losing things. I knew there had been a hammer in there the last time I looked. Was it yesterday or the day before? Why couldn't I find it?

One thing I could almost never find was a decent pair of scissors. I could find safety scissors like the ones kindergarteners used, but when I needed scissors that would actually cut, they were not there. It may have been because Tommy and Pat were young, and scissors were dangerous in the hands of children.

In ninth grade, our English teacher, Mr. Yanzek, handed out scissors so we could cut up our essays. He didn't want us to cut them into little bits but cut out the paragraphs and rearrange them to see if they made better sense in a different order. I held on to my scissors after class like a prize. When I got home, instead of putting them safely in my rolltop desk like I should have, I chucked them into the junk drawer. The next day, they were gone.

My mother had a habit of removing things from my room like rap tapes; a red, yellow, and green Rasta hat; a Michael Jordan T-shirt with a spray paint design that looked too urban for her tastes. She thought I didn't know, but I did. Once these things were gone, I never saw them again; they were not in the trash, my parents' closet, or even in my mother's top drawer. Billy Joel, John Denver, even the Doors—all music I inherited from my parents—those cassettes remained. Michael Jackson was okay, but Bell Biv DeVoe was not. The only thing she did not confiscate was a rock I'd found one day after track practice. It was large, flat, and irregularly shaped. The shape was that of a mysterious continent, and I took it home, feeling its contours in my pocket. I named it my Africa Rock, and it sat on my desk in plain view, unmolested, until I forgot about it. Before that, though, it reminded me that the only black things I could have were the ones only I could see.

A hammer and sharp scissors were actually dangerous, but as far as I knew, my mother never permanently removed them from the house. They weren't confiscated, locked up, or spirited away. After a while, they always turned up. Not so with my cache of teenage trophies.

Instead of writing my email, I decided to work on one of my dissertation chapters.

I retained the trick Mr. Yanzek taught of us cutting up our papers to physically revise them, and as I sat at my desk looking at the printout of my chapter, I realized I needed a pair of scissors.

I rummaged around my desk drawer half-heartedly, knowing already that I didn't have a pair. It was the same kind of junk drawer as the one in the kitchen at Lincoln Boulevard. Everything was in there, but nothing was there when you really needed it.

I thought about the big paper guillotine in the department mail room. There was something satisfying about going in there when no one else was around, slipping an unsuspecting page of an essay under the bar, lining the edges up with the gridlines, and bringing down the blade. It made a gritty slicing sound as it chopped through the imperfect work. I was looking forward to using the guillotine to cut our half-page flyers for the graduate conference—slipping them under the guide rail, lining them up, and chopping them in half with mechanical precision.

The guillotine was the opposite of a pair of scissors in the junk drawer. It was large and heavy; its placement had to be intentional. No one could walk off with the long-bladed device by accident. It multiplied the danger scissors posed but also the fulfillment gained in shaving off a sliver of paper in a perfectly straight line. No chop-chopping crookedly from one end of the page to another. The guillotine was swift and decisive; it got right to the heart of things.

As I sat at my desk dreaming of the guillotine, the image of my younger self, rummaging through the junk drawer at Lincoln Boulevard, returned.

"Mom," I heard myself say as my hands waded through the junk, "where are the scissors?"

"They're in there!" she called from the other side of the kitchen, where she was sweeping a pile of dirt and dog hair into the corner. "Knight!" she yelled at our black Lab, who lumbered through the kitchen, knocking into the heavy oak chairs around the kitchen table, with my four-year-old brother, Tom, chasing him.

The only question I'd ever asked about race in our family was when I was three years old, before my brothers were born.

My dad tanned very dark in the summer, and I remember looking at his tanned arm and realizing his skin was much darker than my mother's and mine.

"Mommy," I asked, "is Daddy black?"

"No," she answered, and she never said another word about it.

Twenty-four years later, I needed a better answer. The only way I felt I could approach this powder keg was to suggest that my dad's grandmother was something other than German. I would ask about the father I knew and hope she told me about the other one.

Fifteen

It was still dark out when my cell phone began to buzz.

When I flipped it open, my mother's voice came through, broken by static. We made some awkward small talk, then she said, "I guess you want to talk about the email you sent me last week."

"Yes," I whispered, trying not to wake Zoran, who was asleep beside me. I glanced at the clock and realized it was 6:30 a.m.

"Before I say anything," she said after a long pause, "tell me if you think we've always loved you."

I began to tear up, and I felt my body grow weak. I knew what was coming.

"Of course," I managed.

She began to cry, and through sobs, she told me a disconnected story about being at a spring break party as a sophomore in college. Someone must have put something in her drink . . . She woke up the next day knowing something had happened, someone had taken advantage of her.

"Are you saying . . . you were raped?" I asked as delicately as I could.

She only cried more and did not answer.

"Was he . . . ," I began, but I couldn't finish the sentence.

"Yes," she said. "He was African American."

"Who was it?" I asked, clambering over Zoran in my underwear, taking the phone into the hallway so as not to wake him.

"I don't know," she said. "I don't remember."

I stood listening to the silence and static on the line.

"Why are you only telling me this now?" I asked.

"Because you asked. I have to go; I'm going to be late for work," she said and hung up.

I stood there shivering in the dark as something came over me I couldn't quite describe.

I'd finally gotten an answer to the question I'd always wanted to ask, but at the same time, I was coming undone.

I suspected I would learn that my biological father was not the man I'd grown up with, but I never expected I was conceived in rape by some guy whose face and name my mother did not remember who might have drugged her. Something didn't make sense, though. If she remembered nothing about him, how could she remember his race?

I had so many questions, but one thing stuck in my head: I'm not a freak of nature. Even if it wasn't the explanation I'd expected or wanted, there was a rational explanation for me after all.

I fell asleep again in a daze, overwhelmed by where the road I'd chosen had taken me.

It was almost noon when Zoran tried to wake me up.

"Time to wake up," he said in Slovak, rocking me back and forth. As he propped himself up on the pillow next to me, his hair fell down around his face and over his shoulders.

"I don't want to," I replied in Slovak, pulling him and the blankets close. His warmth was reassuring. I suddenly felt like I was back in my own world where things made sense, and the phone call that morning seemed like nothing more than a bad dream. I turned my head over on the pillow and squinted up at him through our mingled hair. Dark stubble framed his lips, and his eyes, almost black, sparkled. He saw me looking at him and winked.

"You look like a pirate," I said.

"Of course," he said, brushing some hair back behind his ears. "Slovaks were brigands of the mountains. How else could we have survived?"

While Zoran was in the bathroom, I went over the day's tasks in my head. It felt good to keep my mind busy with mundane thoughts. I had to prepare for the graduate conference on Victorian English literature that weekend, the one for which I'd volunteered.

As a moderator at this new conference, I would have to introduce the presenters, say a few words about the topics, and, when participation flags, come up with informed questions . . . but there was a vague disconnect as my mind slipped back to the revelation I'd received that morning. It wasn't a dream. I tried to incorporate the new information into my store of self-knowledge.

My real father was black and had raped my mother.

When I'd left my meeting with Komunyakaa only a week before, I'd felt a soaring sense of possibility, like I was on the edge of a whole new life. What I knew deep down had been confirmed, but as a result of the worst circumstances possible.

At first, my mother sounded mostly terse and mechanical over the phone. I could tell she'd rehearsed the beginning of what she'd said—if I thought they'd always loved me—but after that she fell apart. The conversation left me stunned and confirmed my worst fears: the asking had hurt her, but the answer hurt both of us. I guess my history was a taboo for a reason.

After my initial shock, I didn't have to put the violence and violation out of my mind; it happened automatically because it was too much for me to deal with. I suddenly felt as if I were looking at myself from the outside. Even as I looked down at my hands, which had always been a few shades darker than my brothers', the color of my own skin seemed foreign. I had always thought of myself as tan, dark, olive, brown—many colors. But never *that color*.

My family identified as Irish and Italian. When I was growing up and people asked me about my nationality, that's what I'd told them I was. My mother's father was the son of Italian immigrants, but her mother was the daughter of immigrants from Greece and Ukraine. The fact that my grandmother was raised in the Greek Orthodox Church or that part of our heritage came from Eastern Europe never entered our family story. I only recently learned that my grandmother's first name was not actually Mary but Dolores. It seemed like my parents and grandparents didn't want our family history to seem complicated so that we could grow up with certainty about who we were in the world.

The main story we were told growing up is that our great-grandmother and great-grandfather came to the United States from Italy without any money. My great-grandmother never learned to speak English, but she raised my grandfather as an American and always kept their small house in Freedom, Pennsylvania, clean. Their first and last names were Americanized at Ellis Island. We didn't learn that our great-grandfather might have had a second family in Michigan or that my great-uncle Ledo, my grandfather's oldest brother, served five years in prison for larceny. We were only supposed to know and care about the good parts of our history. As our mother liked to remind us, we were inheritors of the Roman Empire, the greatest civilization on earth.

The story of the Dunn family, my father told us, was that they were horse thieves who were arrested in eighteenth-century Ireland and given a choice: be sentenced to death or be sent to the New World. The fact that they were most likely sent as indentured servants was never part of the story. One of my father's ancestors was the mayor of Camden, New Jersey. His great-uncle on his mother's side owned a pheasant farm. The stories of our immigrant ancestors were of hard-scrabble endurance, of fearlessness at leaving home to make a life in a new land, and, most of all, of upward mobility. Generation after generation, they worked and scraped their way to the middle class, and it was our duty to go even further.

Being American was important to my parents. One of my father's ancestors fought in the Revolutionary War, and my father used to tell me that meant I was a Daughter of the Revolution, part of a select group of women who could trace their ancestry in this country all the way back to the Colonial era. He did not mention that it was an organization that required official membership or that it was an organization at all; it was simply presented to me as a fact, an honor, and a birthright.

But as it turned out, I was not a Daughter of the Revolution, at least not in the way my father meant it. I was not a Dunn, not the descendant of the brave Irish ruffians to which my father and brothers could lay claim.

My father—my real father—was a mysterious black man, which put me in another category altogether. Without a face, a place, or a name. Did that mean I had no place and no name, too? I knew I was no longer part of the dark Irish clan, but at the moment I lost that heritage, I had no story or lineage with which to replace it. Even though I couldn't admit it, I felt the sting of losing my family's whiteness and felt like I now stood firmly on the other side of a line none of us ever acknowledged, let alone crossed.

When Zoran came out of the bathroom, I wanted to tell him about my mom's phone call, but I hesitated. I still didn't know how I felt about the news. I wanted to know the whole truth, but I also dreaded knowing. So I just kissed him and patted him on the butt as he passed.

In the shower, my brain cells awakened, and I experienced the strangeness and disconnection I was feeling once again.

While I always knew I looked different—as was no doubt obvious to the outside world, including my friends and family—my difference had been a kind of open secret. Our attempts to straighten my hair didn't hide or change how I looked, but the name of what my looks represented was never mentioned.

In high school, my difference was an inside joke between my friends and me. They would say I was the daughter of "Jerome" the milkman and that the racial profile of our school changed depending on how I wore my hair that day. I went along with the joke; after all, I had no straightforward way of articulating the contradictory nature of my position. I had seen enough photos of my parents with me as a newborn and heard the story of my birth enough times not to doubt that they were my "real" parents, but I also knew there was something about my looks—more than just being a dark-featured Italian—that made me different. How could both things be true? It did not help that no one in my family—grandparents, aunts, uncles, and certainly not my brothers or parents—ever remarked about my appearance. My difference—my blackness—was always the elephant in the room, but to us, it all seemed normal. When my brothers' friends asked if I was adopted, they simply responded, "No."

My family was well known and well liked in the community. Ever since we moved to Wexford when I was in kindergarten, my mother had volunteered for everything from lunch lady to Sunday school teacher to PTA to fund-raiser for our varsity sports teams. My father coached our extracurricular sports teams, from my brothers' peewee football and T-ball teams to my softball and basketball teams, even when I was too young and uncoordinated to be any good at sports or care about them.

When I turned twelve, I grew six inches and my coordination improved, helping make me the star athlete I became in high school. In a class of six hundred students, everyone knew me, and I was voted "Most Athletic" every year, despite the fact that there were girls on our varsity diving team who had qualified for the Olympic trials. I was five foot nine by age thirteen and must have looked exotic to the people of Wexford. My appearance prompted comments like, "How old are you? Where are you from? You should be a model!"

Growing up, I lived with a kind of double consciousness. With people who didn't know me, I was exotic, different, possibly black, but definitely *other*. At home with my family, I was a good Irish Italian Catholic girl.

When I got out of the shower, I realized that I no longer had to live with this split sense of self. Finally, I could resolve the contradiction. My difference was no longer a secret. It was like coming out—cause for uneasy celebration. I was both elated at having the burden of identity performance lifted from my conscience but also terrified of what would happen next, of fully stepping into my new identity. So, although it was usually something I did on weekends because it took time to set, I opened the cabinet and reached for my pore-refining charcoal mask. The steam cleared as I applied the blue-black substance to my face, and when I looked in the mirror, my eyes and lips popped out at me from my blackened face under a towel turban.

This is it, I thought. *No more pretending to be something I'm not.*

I could hear the short and long vowels of Slovak in the other room—probably Zoran talking with his mom on the headset. She was in Slovakia, and they talked almost every day. I couldn't remember the last time, before that morning, my mom had called me.

It was like learning to swim without water wings, waking up one day, a grown woman, and learning once and for all that I was black. I knew that having an Italian American mother meant that I was mixed, but I had even less of an idea of what that identity meant. Before I could approach mixed identity, which seemed even more complex and fraught, I needed to integrate my newly effable blackness into my identity.

My first moments of race consciousness were jarring, drowning out every other thought. As I walked around, performing my daily tasks, I was black. I was black as I looked at the sun shining through trees, black as I talked to Zoran on the shuttle to campus. When I walked across the stone courtyard and under the Gothic arch of the Humanities building, I did not do it as a "dark-skinned Italian" but as a black person. I wondered, *Are there certain black ways to do these things that I didn't know about? Will my behavior now change somehow to reflect my official blackness?*

It occurred to me, since I felt inclined to mentally specify that I was black while doing these things, before that I was not simply doing them in some neutral state but as white. It was something I'd never thought about, and it struck me with surprise and shame that my assumed whiteness—despite my persistent doubts—had been a condition of my existence. It also meant that if I felt this way, everyone else must, too. White people were walking around being white without realizing it. Black people were walking around being black, and because of the country we live in, were forced to be aware of it. In this country, minorities were not allowed to forget that they were flying kites, picking out groceries, driving their kids to school, sipping coffee, attending business meetings, and writing books while being whatever hyphenated identity they held, but white people were allowed to think they were just doing these things as human beings. If you were to ask a white person if he was aware that he was being white while gardening or waiting for the bus, he would probably ask you what you meant by that.

I stopped at Small World to get a coffee and stood in line scanning the densely crowded café for people I knew, getting annoyed at the loud banging against the counter that signaled a barista emptying espresso grinds into the trash, and I realized once again that I was doing all this as a black person. My manner had not changed—I still did these routine things in the way I always had, half-consciously, impatiently, thoughts jumping from subject to subject, taking in the sights and smells around me and having positive and negative reactions to them, thinking about what I'd rather be doing, dreading the next day's class preparation and the exhausting tedium of teaching three identical introductory Russian language classes in a row—but the fact of my existence had.

So far, everything was the same—and yet everything was different.

After Small World, I stopped at the graduate lounge in my department to pick up the conference abstracts—the organizers had said they'd leave them in my mailbox. The lounge remained dark, the automatic light not turning on as it should when someone enters the room, and I wondered why it didn't see me.

With the natural light, the old newspapers on the table, the computer parts stacked in the corner, the place felt deserted. I walked to a side wall to look in my mailbox, which was really just a recessed slot among two such rows of slots, and sorted through brightly colored flyers to lectures and events long past, alumni giving requests, and a few old phone bills. (I made a mental note to change my address.) Just as I found the abstracts and was about to take them out of the brown, string-tied envelope, Frank, the language instructor for whom I'd been a teaching assistant, walked in.

For some reason, his flaming hair and beard, his tie that only hung halfway down his shirtfront, and his self-important junior-faculty manner particularly annoyed me at that moment. I pretended to be deeply engaged in my abstracts, hoping he'd ignore me, but he stuck out his potbelly (perhaps not intentionally) in collegial recognition when he saw me.

"*Okh! Zdravstvuite*, Sara Robertovna," he said. "Have you picked up Monday's homework?"

"No," I said, angling to avoid a conversation he would inevitably steer toward the linguistic specificity of Russian participles or the deterioration of university a cappella singing. He was American—from Boston—but liked to keep up the language teacher façade even outside the classroom, which I found incredibly creepy and unnerving. In that moment, I noticed that everything about Frank was very, *very* white. As I registered this, I realized that, in addition to being annoyed, I also felt defensive.

Though I always tried to avoid conversation with Frank, this time I didn't even smile. I tried to edge past him, my envelope held in front of my chest, but he stood resolutely between me and the door, sweating a little.

"Sara Robertovna," he said again with a false nasality that made my skin crawl. In Russian, Sarah is written and pronounced without the H, a point he never failed to mention, even though I had been writing my name in Russian for years. The patronymic Robertovna, synthesized from my father's first name, which he insisted on using "for the sake of cultural authenticity in the classroom," as he put it, seemed like an especially cruel joke in this moment. "Your family's Italian, right?"

I did not know what he was getting at, but I had to pause because, technically, that was true. I waited in silence, trying to look defiant, although I wasn't used to not smiling—even at Frank—and it made me uncomfortable, like I was the one being rude.

"Last semester, McGavaran TA-ed with me," he continued. "I bet we looked like two stuffed shirts!" He fingered the paper cup in his hands but did not throw it in the trash. "At least this semester, they have one instructor who's less male and less white than me. Looks good for the department, too. Russian doesn't get many instructors like you." He lingered, smiling, but my lack of response put us both ill at ease. Was he trying to give me a compliment?

"Look, Frank," I said, focusing on a spot above his head and shifting my weight forward, "I am not *less* anything. I have a student waiting for me downstairs. I have to go." My heart was pounding, and my only instinct was to *get out*. I pushed past him, but I sensed he was watching me, and I tried not to run down the corridor.

Just before I went down the steps, he called, his voice still too near, "Don't forget to take the homework!"

Downstairs, the café, with its red walls and silver tables, seemed like another planet. The place swarmed with students, and every seat on the black couch circling the room was occupied by these vagabonds and their giant sacks. The lights and noise were dizzying, and I had to shoulder through the line forming at the counter to get a seat.

I finally unpacked the abstracts. They did not contain the authors' names but were simply marked for the panel entitled "The Voice of Sense." There were only three papers: "Sense and Sensible Nonsense in the Poetry of William Butler Yeats," "No Sense Is Good Sense: The Open Poem and Postmodern Receptivity," and "The Dramatic Monologue and the Divine Auditor." *What a bunch of bullshit*, I thought, disappointed that I could not even drown my thoughts in them. I got up to get coffee and suddenly realized that I was like one chip in a really big cookie. Looking around, I noted a few other chips. Funny, I thought, that I never noticed.

As I read the abstracts, my frustration and anger mounted. Not only were they poorly written, they were completely irrelevant. Why should I, as a black person, care about Yeats and postmodern receptivity? And what the hell is the Divine Auditor? I read:

In the nineteenth century, speakers of dramatic monologues address themselves to God, the Divine Auditor, because they cannot reveal their thoughts to one another.

I slammed the papers down in disgust; around me, the din of the café was deafening. The topic was so English. So white. No black person would ever think of a topic like this because the inability to communicate openly was a white problem. Black people had no problem speaking their minds. Just that morning, the guy cleaning the women's bathroom tried to pick me up!

I was pained that I had to concentrate on these ridiculous abstracts when I had much more pressing concerns. Ingrid, a fellow grad student in my program, saw a free spot at my table and came over. Sveta and I didn't like Ingrid, and we didn't invite her to the grad conference. The awkwardness was palpable.

"Hallo!" she said, the *ha* as breathy as her pixie cut and freshwater pearls. "There is no room today, ah?" She unbelted her skinny trench coat and slid into the seat opposite.

"Has Frank seemed strange to you lately?" I asked.

She tried to suppress a smile, but failed.

"You mean he finally tried to ask you out?" She asked this as if it were a reasonable question.

Even though I usually do not blush, I felt heat rising in my face. "What are you talking about?" I asked, and it was not a question as much as a demand.

"You haven't noticed? The whole department knows!" She laughed, and I realized what was stunning about Ingrid, besides her creamy skin and doe eyes, was that her voice, with its killer accent, could become very husky and low. "Remember the little birthday cake, the Valentine card in your mailbox, the Orthodox Easter card? You are not even Orthodox, *ja*?" She had a point, but this was not what interested me.

"He said something racially offensive to me today," I said, trying to convey the gravity of the situation.

"What?" Ingrid said in disbelief. "What is your race?"

"I'm black," I said as if I were used to saying this, as if it were self-evident.

She looked at me and thought for a moment. "No, you look not so black. Greek, maybe, or Creole—from Martinique."

"My mother is part Greek, actually," I said, but she wouldn't let me finish.

"Oh, so you are mixed; that is different. See Zoran over there?" I looked to see Zoran at a far booth with his laptop and headset and wondered why she'd spotted him before I did.

"In Slovakia, they are all mixed. There is no such thing as 'Slovak.'

He, for instance, is quarter Czech, quarter Austrian, quarter Hungarian, and quarter Slovak." She squinted across the room at him, reckoning. His hair was down and collar undone as if he'd just blown in from the high seas.

"He is very tan," she continued. "He looks more Hungarian than Slovak."

"How do you know so much about Zoran?" I asked, as an inkling of suspicion dawned.

"Oh, nothing," she said. "I only see him at the international dinners."

My stomach gurgled acidly as I sipped my coffee. "It had better only be international dinners," I said, looking, unsmiling, into her big, velvety eyes.

"Well," she said, her voice low, "Central Europeans are naturally close. We have a lot in common, much more so than with Americans."

"That's a lie," I said. "Zoran said himself that no one would speak to him in Berlin. He said no one hates Eastern Europeans more than Germans."

"I am from Austria," Ingrid said. She picked up her trench coat and, before making her exit, added, "Maybe you should not forget Frank, ah? Americans with interest in language have much to talk about."

"Slut," I said under my breath, but she was already gone.

Fuming, I looked over again at Zoran, who had not noticed anything of this little scene. He had his headset on and his expression was concentrated, a sure sign he was talking to his mother. *Again? How many times does a grown man need to talk to his mother during a single day?* This was not normal, not even for him. Still, I collected my bag, coffee, and papers and elbowed through the crowd to his table.

"Hey," I said, and he waved in a way that both greeted me and signaled that I shouldn't talk. I sank into the leather booth.

He took off his headset, but a worried expression lingered around his temples.

"How are you?" he said, giving me a quick kiss. Without waiting for the answer, he handed me a large stack of papers. "You will correct this for me?" he asked, and I saw his latest chapter on Aristotle's moral psychology.

"What am I, your slave?" I nearly yelled this, but it was lost in the din.

I expected him to see that I was truly upset and apologize, but instead, he brightened and said, "Yes, why don't you be my slave?" He held me against his shoulder, stroking my mass of curly hair. "I promise to feed you—one warm meal each day. And not to sell you for one year! What do you say?"

I pushed him away, knocking over his coffee, which splattered over his shirt, his chapter, his laptop. He jumped to salvage the machine, bewildered, and this gave me unexpected glee.

"Guess you can't call your mom back," I chided. "Or maybe you'd rather talk to Ingrid?"

"*Ježiš Maria,*" he said as he picked up his laptop, tipping some liquid out. He was cursing in Slovak, but stopped when he saw my face. "What is wrong?" he asked.

It was then that I realized I was standing above him, tears streaming down my face. I took a wad of coffee napkins and blew my nose. When I wiped my eyes, I was startled to see black rub off and realized my mascara must be destroyed.

"I bet I look awful," I said, trying to laugh.

"Yes, you look bad," Zoran said as I sat down.

"You know," I said, calming down a bit, "this morning, while you were asleep—"

"I know," he cut in. "I heard you. You are not so quiet as you think." His face softened, and I leaned against his arm.

"She lied to me," I whispered into his shirt.

"Not lie," he said. "She just didn't want to hurt you."

"What do you know about it?" I said, suddenly angry as I grabbed more coffee napkins from the table to wipe my face.

"While you were in the shower," he said, continuing to blot his laptop, "on the phone, my mother told me she has cancer. She has known for one month."

"But you talk to her every day," I said. "That's awful! Why didn't she tell you earlier?"

"She knows that if I leave to Slovakia before the semester is over, I cannot return to the US. It is not in my visa. My father is now in Austria." He got up to get more napkins. When he came back, he said, "I am sorry. In ancient Greece, they have slaves, but I forget that about this Americans cannot joke."

The day of the conference, I woke at 8:00 and there were puffy bags under my eyes. Outside it was cold, and the wind crept into my coat seams, leaving me feeling exposed. Rain assailed the windows, roofs, and pavement. My old umbrella soon soaked through, fat drops matting my hair in sections, frizzing it in others, undermining my professional look. My heels, which were also for the occasion, stumbled through puddles, and before I reached the car, gravel found its way into my shoe, grinding against the damp balls of my feet. In the car, I switched the windshield wipers on, and for a moment I was not sure where I was going.

As if by accident, I found Adams Hall, the auditorium where the conference was taking place. The organizers—other doctoral students like myself—were glad I'd come early, as they frantically arranged bottled water on the refreshments table, stretched too-small trash bags over the mouths of the trash cans provided by Event Services, and called Maintenance to locate the auditorium's light switch. Soon the presenters arrived, walking down the short hallway to the auditorium's lobby, shaking rain off coats and umbrellas, nervously smiling or pretending to look over the heads of the group of us waiting to greet them and give them name tags.

By 9:00, most of the participants had arrived, and I had greeted, tagged, and offered coffee to the authors of the first two papers on my panel. The author of "Sense and Sensible Nonsense" was a large bearded man in his late thirties wearing a sweater vest and suit coat. He brushed a hand over a receding wave of chestnut hair as he chatted with me conspiratorially.

"Yeats is so much better if you read him with an Irish brogue," he confided, pronouncing the *o*'s in dialect.

Thank goodness for name tags, I thought, chatting with the author of "No Sense Is Good Sense," whose waist-length locks, thick-rimmed glasses, and floor-trailing skirt seemed to be common features of several conference members.

The first panel began at 9:30, and as we filed into the auditorium, I scanned the participants and lobby area for any sign of my third author. Our panel would begin after lunch, the last of three, so in theory, the missing author had plenty of time. However, it was considered bad form to show up only for one's own talk, not taking part in other discussions. Perhaps, I noted to myself, there was a reason besides English dourness the author chose to write on monologue.

The organizers were nervous because they'd already had one last-minute cancellation that morning, which shortened the second panel to two papers. One lame duck panel was fine, they said, but the afternoon would drag on endlessly if the final panel was too short to fill the allotted time. I told them the nasty weather was probably at fault and our author would turn up any time. They hoped so, they whispered, as the keynote address began.

After two long panels and lunch, which I could barely touch for the knot forming in my stomach, the author of "The Divine Auditor" was still missing. As the participants excused themselves for a final bathroom break before the last panel, one of the organizers came up to me.

"How long is your introduction?" she asked. "Do you think you can improvise a bit on the themes of the last paper so we'll have something to talk about?"

"Sure," I said, digging through my conference folder for the introduction I'd written. "I'm sure I can . . ."

My sentence trailed off as I realized the clock was about to strike 1:30, and the participants, minus the few who'd sneaked off after lunch, were making their way back into the auditorium. I searched my brain for any tidbit of nineteenth-century monologue trivia that may have been accidentally stored there, when I felt someone touch my arm. I looked up to see a woman of towering height, taller than I, beautiful, with long microbraids tied back in a scarf, a few stray ones falling around her shiny, dark face. She smiled so that I could see her white teeth and mouthed, "I'm so sorry."

"Are you—the Divine Auditor?" I said before I realized what I was asking. I was completely floored by her appearance and felt an uncomfortable sweat—the kind that stinks—seeping into my armpits.

"Yes, I'm Celia," she said, taking out her papers as we entered the auditorium.

I took my seat next to Celia at the table in front of the audience and introduced the speakers. I felt as if a strong hand had gripped my spinal column inside my neck and that that force alone was keeping me upright, turning my head from side to side, nodding it during each talk with scholarly approval. I could no longer think of anything but my own assumptions and how wrong I'd been. *She's black*, I thought. *What must she think of me?* I felt like a fraud, just another white person who only knew how to relate to blackness through stereotypes. I felt the hand's grip tighten as I listened to Celia deliver an even-toned lecture on God as listener in the late-nineteenth century. She was saying:

God hears the kind of talk that goes on in the hidden places of the greedy heart. What God therefore demands is complete integrity and transparency.

To whom was I accountable now, and why did I care? To myself, to my mother, to this woman who suddenly had become my new God? Her polished mahogany arm lay close to mine on the table, and even though my throat was parched, I did not reach for my water for fear my hand would tremble violently, that I would offend her by unleashing an acrid stench, or that I would grab her arm and begin stroking it violently, press it to my face to feel its blackness. I wanted to know what real blackness felt like, not the confused phony state of whatever I was. I wanted to know her secrets, feel the warmth radiating off her skin. I wanted to be inside her dark, gorgeous body, to be inside her mind and know what she knew, to be what she was.

I asked the audience if they had questions for the panelists and tried to moderate the ensuing exchange while keeping my arms rigidly at my sides. *What does she think of me?* I wondered again. *Is she glad there's another black woman here? A sister?* My concluding comments, which came from a place other than my brain, which was on autopilot, even elicited a few laughs. After scattered applause, the crowd quickly dispersed, leaving only the organizers and the panelists who were gathering their papers.

I wanted to say something to Celia, some expression or acknowledgment of our shared connection amid the sea of whiteness. I shook hands with the other presenters and followed her out into the lobby.

"I really enjoyed your paper," I ventured as she put on her coat to leave.

"Thanks," she said.

Looking around and dropping my voice a little, I added, "It's always the same at these things, though—not one other black person in sight."

"You must know what it's like, too," she said to me sympathetically, "to be a Latina in . . . what's your field?"

"Russian," I choked.

"Oh," she said disinterestedly, suddenly reaching in her bag as it sounded an electronic version of *Peer Gynt*. "I've got to go. It was nice meeting you." She took one more look at me, a little more searching perhaps, as if she were about to say something else, but I could not meet her gaze, and I, too, began riffling through my bag, pretending I'd gotten a call.

Sixteen

After the phone conversation with my mother, my parents decided that it would be a good idea for the family to get together and talk about the revelation, as it came to be called. I still had many questions about what happened and who my father was. My parents would come to Princeton for Thanksgiving. Patrick, who was a first-year graduate student in the University of Chicago Divinity School, could make it. Tom, who was a sophomore at Virginia Tech, would drive up from Pittsburgh with my parents.

In the meantime, I tried to keep up with my busy schedule and attend doctor and therapist appointments for my worsening health. Grad school was stressful on its own, but the emotional stress I was dealing with started to break me down. I could hardly eat. I kept drinking coffee even though it made me feel awful; I needed the caffeine to keep going.

From the outside, I looked fine. I was slim and well groomed. It was easy for me to hide how I felt, to tamp down difficult emotions and tell everyone I was fine. But on the pillow every morning, I noticed more and more hair, and in the shower, clumps of loose hair slid down my back and shoulders, making me shiver in disgust, collecting in spidery masses around the drain. My eyelashes thinned, and I lost weight from my inability to eat. My skin became ashy and my nails brittle.

My schedule was formidable at the best of times, but now I struggled to keep up with basic daily tasks and willed myself not to collapse. I began to panic. *I can't do it,* I thought, admitting my limitations for perhaps the first time in my life. I emailed Frank and told him that I needed a couple of days off from teaching, hoping, for once, that his predisposition toward me would work in my favor. His reply dashed all hope.

"This is highly unusual," he wrote. "I will have to consult with Ivor and get back to you."

As soon as he mentioned Ivor Savich, the director of Graduate Studies, my heart sank. During my time at Princeton, I worked closely with Professor Savich. I performed well in his classes and even served as his research assistant one summer, but for some reason, despite my efforts, he never took me seriously. I envisioned his hawklike brows furrowing as he read Frank's email, chalking my request up to one more example of my unreliability. Still in a panic, I emailed Professor Savich my own explanation. I was shaking as I pressed Send.

His reply came half an hour later.

"You cannot take time off teaching; it doesn't work that way. Your issue isn't going away, so you'll just have to get used to it. I.S."

The next morning at 8:45 a.m. as I entered the classroom, Professor Savich was there waiting for me. "I wanted to make sure you showed up," he said. He stood outside the door and watched me teach the entire class. By the time the students dispersed and my second group of students began to arrive, he was gone.

• • •

Almost all my friends in the doctoral program practiced some form of self-harm.

My form of self-harm was exercising for hours each day, binge eating, and using laxatives to purge what I'd eaten. My behavior was never formally diagnosed as bulimia, but the cycle of binging, purging, and nervously weighing myself each day kept me in a state of constant panic and added to the dysfunction I already felt. No matter how slim and toned I became, I was never thin enough. On two occasions that year, I ended up in the emergency room for exhaustion and dehydration.

I didn't think I had an eating disorder; I just thought I was overworked. After I grudgingly told my friends that I'd been to the ER a second time, Sveta made me sign a contract stating that I would take better care of myself, eat healthier, and cut out performance-enhancing supplements. I still didn't think I had a problem, but they said, "Well, just in case."

After being forced to teach Russian 101 when I could barely get out of bed, I was too burned out to exercise, and I only avoided eating because I couldn't digest most food.

I didn't want to burden my friends with my issues at the moment, but I needed to talk to someone. I'd been seeing a therapist since my breakup the previous year, and our sessions focused on how my relationship with a graduate student from Rutgers who was a neuroscientist and a bodybuilder had affected my body image, eating, and self-esteem issues.

The therapist was a woman of Indian descent, with a dark complexion and long, straight hair. She was forthright but patient and coached me through some hard times. I didn't have an appointment scheduled that week, and it was usually difficult to schedule an appointment at McCosh Health Center on short notice. I feared being handed a clipboard and sheet to fill out detailing my health concerns. Most of the questions focused on physical health, but there was a section at the end that screened for depression. Every time I went to the health center, even if I couldn't get an appointment with the therapist, I was given one of these sheets, and every time, I circled "nearly every day" for questions that asked how often I:

Feel depressed or hopeless
Have little interest in doing things
Have little energy
Have trouble sleeping
Feel like a failure or disappointment to those around you
Have thoughts you would be better off dead or of harming
    yourself in some way

The health center never followed up with me. It felt like their attitude was: According to this questionnaire, you have severe depression. Good luck!

Graduate students were allowed twenty free therapy appointments per year through the university. After that, we had to fend for ourselves.

I climbed the two flights of stairs to the counseling office.

"I need to make an appointment with Dr. Ramsey," I almost whispered, inclining my head toward the receptionist.

"We don't have any openings until next month," she said, glancing at the computer screen.

"It's urgent—I need to see her as soon as possible." I paused. "It's an emergency."

I fidgeted with the strap on my bag. It was difficult for me to get these last words out, and my voice must have wavered a bit because the receptionist finally looked up at me as if to gauge whether or not I looked like someone who needed emergency counseling.

I wasn't disheveled; I wasn't screaming or crying or shaking or displaying any of the outward behaviors that the media teaches us constitute a panic attack or someone having a mental breakdown. All my life, I'd cultivated a strong, calm outward demeanor even in the toughest of situations. Growing up, it had been considered weak to display any signs of emotion. I knew it was better to act tough, so that's what I usually did.

My composure did not help me now because I simply did not know how to convey my desperation in a way that would convince this gate-keeper that I was on the brink of disaster. Expressing difficult emotions was not easy for me; my reactions to emotions—even pleasant ones—weren't spontaneous. Inside, I felt numb. Yet that numbness betokened a deep panic. My inability to foresee what lay on the other side of my steadily disintegrating sense of self made it all the more terrifying.

"Please," I whispered. "I need to see her as soon as possible." I tried to make myself cry, to show any kind of emotion to match the tumultuous state I was in, but I was too used to holding back. My voice came out evenly; my request sounded nonchalant.

"What is this regarding?" the receptionist asked.

"It's hard to explain—it's family related . . ." Should I have said I was suicidal? I didn't want to lie, and I didn't feel like I should have to lie to get the support I needed in that moment.

"Well," the attendant said reluctantly, "she has a window today after lunch." She picked up the phone, pressed a button, and had a short conversation with the person on the other end. "It's only for twenty minutes."

"That's fine," I responded eagerly.

"Have a seat, and I'll call you when she's back in."

I took a seat in the featureless waiting room. Some pamphlets about STD awareness hung in holders on the wall. The health center newsletter was the only reading material on the side table. I picked one up and was about to leaf through it when I heard my name.

It was darker than usual in Dr. Ramsey's office, with only a small table lamp giving off light. It may have been to create a sense of intimacy, or to convey that she was not meant to be receiving patients at that time. At any rate, after some awkward small talk, I explained why I had needed to see her so quickly. I detailed the conversation with my mother as best I could and tried to explain that although I had always suspected I was African American, I still didn't know how to process this change in identity, what it meant for myself and my family. I told her how my mother told me I was conceived.

"Wow," she said, looking at me intensely. It seemed like an unprofessional response. Weren't doctors and therapists supposed to have heard everything? I just wanted some assurance that I wasn't crazy or making a big deal out of nothing; that I was indeed experiencing a life-altering change. I couldn't articulate any of this at the time, I only had the distinct feeling of coming unmoored. She got up and turned the overhead light on, as if noticing for the first time that the room was darker than it ought to be. I sat on the stiff chair, hugging a throw pillow to keep from shaking. While she sat back down, I waited.

"It's just that—you look so much darker to me now," she finally said, playing with the silver bracelets on her wrist. I didn't hear the rest of what she said. She asked some questions; I responded automatically. Soon the twenty minutes were up. I thanked her, not knowing what else to do, and left the office more bewildered than when I'd gone in.

Seventeen

My family arrived Wednesday afternoon and booked themselves into an extended-stay Hilton on Route 1 not far from the university. Even though I was dreading the reunion, I was more than happy to get out of my drafty house with its paper-thin walls and reclusive roommate.

The wind had picked up some, but it was still mild. Most of the leaves had fallen, but the air did not yet carry the chill of winter. Clouds in the November sky hung low and lower, it seemed, over the Hilton. Even though the heater in my car was turned all the way up, I felt cold as I pulled into the parking lot, unsure of what awaited me.

It would be the first time I'd faced my mother since our phone conversation, the first time our family would openly acknowledge my different father and race. After twenty-seven years of all of us avoiding the issue, I did not know what to expect. How would my parents handle the conversation? How would Patrick and Tom react? With the personal crises my friends were going through, I hadn't talked to them about what was going on between my family and me.

I walked through the lobby, feeling the eyes of the desk clerk follow me as I went toward the elevator. Maybe I imagined it, but I had the sense of not feeling welcome. I knocked on the door of my parents' suite, and my dad opened it.

The familiar sight of him, with his tan skin, slightly grown-out black hair, and dark green L.L.Bean coat one size too large almost convinced me that everything was normal and that their visit was nothing more than a family gathering for the holidays. But the thought lasted only for a moment, and even when he greeted me with his customary "Hey, Bean," the tension did not give way.

My dad gave me a big hug, holding me for longer than usual, which made me even tenser. I greeted Pat, who, at six foot one, was skinnier and taller than my dad. I noticed his thick dark hair and beard were growing out, and he was wearing a baggy plaid shirt. We hugged, again for longer than usual. Tom also gave me a hug. He was six foot two and also a bit shaggy. I was glad he and Pat were there; it made me feel like I had allies. Finally, I saw my mother. She looked smaller than I remembered, but everything else about her was the same: pursed lips with neutral lipstick, sensible silver jewelry, her lightened hair cut in a long bob with bangs. She was wearing a V-necked sweater over a button-down blouse and dark pants, and Dansko clogs. We all stood in the entry of the anonymous room, the moment lingering.

My mother and I hugged, and I felt uneasy. After our first conversation, I'd felt like she was the victim, but now, standing in the hotel room, I felt she'd betrayed me. She made a decision twenty-seven years ago and kept it a secret. Didn't she know that eventually the truth would come out? Didn't she think about what it would do to me?

My dad led us to the living room, and we all sat down, my brothers and I on the hard sofa, my parents in each of the chairs opposite.

My dad was talking, not my mother. He told us in a grave voice that I had a different father and that I was half-black. With a shake of his head, he swore he had nothing to do with all this and that it was the first he was hearing of it himself.

Pat nodded thoughtfully. Tom was silent.

My mom remained silent.

I felt as if I were hearing the conversation from a great distance, their talk muted and faint.

My mother brought out a big red velvet heart-shaped box with gold trim from her bag. Shakespeare's words were embroidered on the top with golden thread: *Love is not love that alters when it alteration finds.*

"I wanted you to see that I was happy then," she said, handing me the box. I opened it and took out a framed photo of my parents and me when I was about one year old. It looked like it was taken in an instant photo booth; their heads were pressed together, and my dad was holding me up between them. They sported big toothy smiles and seemed happy to capture a moment of togetherness with their young family. I could see that I was noticeably darker than they were and that my curly hair and facial features didn't match up with theirs. It was nice to see how young and exuberant they were, so happy to be parents at twenty-one and twenty-two years old. But how could they not have wondered why I was so dark? Why my cute button nose in no way resembled their longer, high-ridged ones?

We spent the night fighting. I asked my mother these questions, and she said they just didn't think about it.

"Don't you understand we just fell in love with you? We knew you were ours and wanted to take care of you the best we could."

I asked her if she understood how I felt to have been robbed of my identity growing up, or why raising me "the best they could" didn't include acknowledging or celebrating my black heritage.

"What should we have done?" she mocked. "Eat fried chicken and watermelon and talk like this?"

She made some crude rapper gestures and did her best impression of a ghetto accent. She didn't think it was offensive; to her, that's what black meant. Her idea of blackness was just an amalgam of stereotypes and violence.

She told me I already had an identity: Wasn't that good enough for me?

I locked myself in the bathroom and cried. I had a brief flash of doing the same thing at my fourteenth birthday party when Rachel Turner told me I was a snob.

Outside, I could hear Pat and Tom arguing with my mom, their voices rising angrily. My dad knocked on the door and implored me to come out, but I didn't answer. I always suspected my mom had no interest in anyone's culture but her own. I remembered us walking through the mall when I was young and seeing a woman wearing a sari walking toward us. As she passed, my mom whispered to me, "If she wants to be in America, she should dress like it."

I couldn't understand how my dad, who seemed so much worldlier and more open-minded than my mom could have gone along with this. Was it even about worldliness? Or did the rules change when it came to one's own family?

"It has nothing to do with me," he kept saying through the door. "This is between you and your mother."

All I could think about was how little this seemed to mean to my parents. They were upset because I was upset, but if they had their way, we would have never discussed the subject at all.

After I got the call from my mom, my life changed into "before" and "after." Not only did things change for me from that moment on-ward, I now saw the past in the light of a fiercely kept family secret.

I heard my mother yelling through the door, "If this is the worst thing that's happened in your life, you should be grateful!"

I didn't know if she meant that I should be grateful that what hap-pened to her didn't happen to me, or if she meant that learning what I had just learned should not be a big deal. I didn't think she under-stood the kind of rupture I was experiencing.

The news made me question all my experiences with my family. The birthdays, holidays, family dinners, summer vacations, basketball practices, games, camps, and tournaments—everything we did to-gether now felt like a lie, like the whole time an untruth was hovering around us we'd all agreed to ignore. I just kept thinking, if my race or biological father didn't matter, as my mother insisted, then why did it need to be a secret? Why couldn't we have the same experi-ences as a family without pretending I was white? If my parents wanted to spare me the pain or confusion of knowing I had a differ-ent biological father when I was young, why didn't they tell me when I was older?

When I came out of the bathroom with tears still streaming down my face, my dad tried to ameliorate the situation by saying, "It's kind of like you're adopted."

"But you said you didn't know!" I yelled back. "You can't adopt a child by accident!"

It was too late for them to frame our situation as adoption. During our conversation, they never said, "We wanted to wait until you were ready," or "We were waiting for you to ask."

My mother had tears streaming down her face, too.

"I wish I'd never told you," she kept saying.

I began to feel like my denial of my race all these years was more about protecting my parents than protecting myself and that deep down I always knew it. My mother instilled in us how much she sacrificed to be a mother, dropping out of college, staying home with us throughout our childhoods, never having a job or life of her own until she was older. She told us what a great father we had, and it was true. She said she wished she'd had a father like that. Growing up, I saw my parents—especially my mother—the same way I saw Jesus: selfless martyrs who only cared about others. I felt loyal and indebted to them. I could never pay them back for all they'd done for us, but I felt compelled to dedicate my life to trying.

Feeling this way, how could I have forced the issue of my difference as a child, or even as a teenager? It was difficult enough for me to do now. The subject of my essay for college applications was about how my mother, like Jesus, set a moral example for me and how I wanted to do my best to embody that spirit of honesty and sacrifice.

Now, that all seemed like a bad joke. It was still true, but at the same time, it wasn't.

I knew that from their point of view, they were protecting me from an ugly truth that could have affected my self-esteem, especially in the world in which we lived. It could have made me feel more isolated among my peers; my identity crisis could have come much sooner. Would I have been able to resolve it and adapt?

"When I found out I was pregnant, I was twenty years old," my mother said. "I didn't want a child, and I was scared. I thought about having an abortion, but I just couldn't do it. If your father hadn't married me, I would have given you away." She paused. "I just couldn't raise you as a single mother. We would have been outcasts. Don't you see that it doesn't matter?" she implored.

"After everything you just said," I yelled, "how could it not matter?"

"All that matters is that we loved you and wanted the best for you. You think being black is more important than that? It doesn't mean anything! It's all made up!"

Her tone was desperate but still had an edge.

"I can't believe you really think this is important," she continued, her voice steadying. "You have no idea how happy we were to raise you. You were so much fun! It was so gratifying watching you learn and grow into a smart, beautiful, young woman, and we made sure you had all the opportunities we never did. Isn't that what's really important? I wish someone had done all that for me when I was growing up. That's how I based everything I did as a parent: to do the things no one had done for me."

I always felt my parents loved and supported me. They celebrated my successes and made me feel special. In the face of that feeling, I didn't know how to explain the emptiness, betrayal, and loss I felt. It felt like I was being told that only one of these things—either my race or their love—could matter.

My mom went on to insist that she didn't know I was black.

"Daddy is dark," she said. "He's darker than you. Don't you see? There was always an explanation."

She wanted me to believe her, and maybe she wanted to believe that herself, but when she talked about knowing she would have to give me away unless my father married her, I knew she feared her parents would not have accepted her as a young single mother with a black child.

I knew the circumstances of my conception made it even more difficult for her to accept my identity as part black. She wanted to forget—and had forgotten—the person who conceived me. She wanted that whole moment in her life to vanish, and it until now had.

Now here I was bringing back painful memories when I should have just been grateful for the life I had. It made me feel like the bad guy, an advocate for someone who had harmed her. Was it really impossible for her to separate my identity from the person she wanted to forget, or did she have to bury that part of me in order to love and care for me the way she did? Could some lines simply not be crossed?

My parents gave me a culture and an identity. Growing up, I knew who I was and where I belonged. We built our family together. For them, that was enough.

As I grew, I realized there was more to me—not less—than the person my family recognized. Identity is all the aspects that make up a person, and the facts of who I was were more complicated than my family wanted to admit. Identity is culture and affinity—characteristics I had that were shaped by my environment and ones I possessed independent of it. I was Irish, Italian, and African American. All those heritages were a part of me whether my parents believed that or not. The part of me my parents wanted to deny was the part that everyone saw.

Black, African American, mixed, biracial. What did these identities mean to me? I had a whole set of questions to figure out, and I knew my parents couldn't help me.

As we argued, Pat took my side. He was as outraged as I was that they kept this secret from us and felt a deep sense of betrayal. He talked about telling his friends no when they asked if his sister was adopted. He and I—and probably Tommy, too—always had to field questions about why I looked different, but no one had the courage to confront my parents about it. Didn't they realize they forced us into a position that made it look like we were lying?

Besides my racial identity, there was an even bigger elephant in the room. Our entire discussion begged a question we had so far avoided: Who was my biological father?

"How could you even ask that?" she said in disbelief. "Why is it important?"

I said I had a right to know and that it was completely natural and rational for a person to want to know who his or her father was.

It hit her like a slap in the face.

"Haven't I done enough?" she asked. "How stupid do you have to be to really believe that's important?"

One of the photos in the Valentine's Day box showed my mom and her friends in a dorm room in their pajamas. They were laughing, all piled on the bed. I recognized some faces in the photo as friends my mother had known since grade school. A couple of the faces were unfamiliar.

"Who took this picture?" my dad asked. His question was unexpected.

"Why are you asking me that?" replied my mother, exasperated.

Suddenly, I wasn't the focus of the argument. The air between them was tense with something unsaid.

"Sherry was dating someone black," he said, pointing at one of the unfamiliar girls in the photo. "Wasn't it—"

I didn't hear what he said because I was lost in a cloud of thoughts and emotions, but whatever it was hit a nerve, and mother screamed at him in response, "Why are you accusing me? Aren't I allowed to have friends? I can't believe you would bring that up!"

After being shouted down, my father gave up.

We were all exhausted, and my parents decided to go to bed.

Eighteen

"What was that about?" I asked my brothers as soon as the bedroom door closed.

"I don't know," Pat said. He and Tom seemed as dazed as I was, with as many questions and no good answers.

"Tara has been interning on a film in the city, and it just came out," I said.

"What's the film?"

"It's a Jim Jarmusch film; I don't know what it's about. She said she got to hang out with Bill Murray on set. It's called *Broken Flowers*. Want to watch it?"

"Sure," he said. Tom also nodded.

We turned on the TV and clicked Pay-Per-View.

The film opened on a black screen and the rich clicking of a manual typewriter.

An envelope, bright pink, drops into a mailbox and makes the rounds through an automated mail sorting facility as moody surf rock plays. A mail carrier walks through a quiet neighborhood past a stand of shade trees, a kid wearing a helmet riding a bike. Dappled light all around; the picture of suburban tranquility.

The first house we see has blue siding. Black children are playing in the front yard. A child's swing hangs from a tree; a small basketball hoop, a mini table and chairs set for tea, and other toys are scattered around the yard and driveway. The front door stands open; funky music plays within. The children laugh; fall leaves swish beneath their running feet. A truck and a van stand parked at angles in the driveway.

As the mail carrier passes a thicket of high, well-groomed shrubbery, the boisterous sounds fade, and the chirping of birds in the silence grows louder.

She enters a wide, manicured lawn and begins to walk toward the front door. The camera zooms out to take in the grand scale of the house as she walks up to a door flanked by stone columns.

In the living room, a beautiful woman in an expensive-looking pink suit, played by Julie Delpy, is breaking up with Don, played by Bill Murray, who wears a black tracksuit with red stripes. He seems confused but not upset by what's happening. She asks him if he wants a family.

"Is that what you want?" he asks.

"I don't know what I want," she says. "I just know I want to figure it out on my own."

As she walks out, we feel Don's apathy; he got himself into a rut years ago and doesn't have the energy or desire to change.

Afterward, we see him sitting on a sleek leather couch. The pink letter drops through the mail slot; its bright color stands out among the neutral tones of the high-end mid-century modern furniture around him.

Bill Murray reads the letter out loud:

"Dear Don,

"Sometimes life brings some strange surprises. It's been almost twenty years since we've seen each other, but now there's something I need to tell you. Years ago, after our story ended, I discovered I was pregnant. I decided to go through with the pregnancy, and I had a baby—a son. Your son. I decided to raise him by myself because our time together had come to a close."

She tells him her son is nineteen and has gone on a road trip to find his father.

My brother looked at me, and we both giggled.

"I swear to God I didn't know this is what the film was about!" I said.

It felt like an uncanny coincidence that the film was about a man learning he has a son who has set off to find him. The letter contains no names, no return address—no real information. To me, that made it feel like something was off; why go through the trouble of writing someone this kind of letter if you didn't want him to know the details? The letter writer didn't even know if she had Don's correct address but decided to write anyway. How did she even know he was the father?

Don's neighbor Winston, played by Jeffrey Wright, helps him make a list of his past lovers and persuades him to go on a journey of his own to find out who the mother is and, hopefully, meet his son. Even though I didn't want to admit it, the scene made me wonder if there was someone out there looking for me. Don seemed to be searching for meaning in his life; he didn't have a family and he wasn't sure he even wanted one. Maybe he felt a sense of responsibility, or maybe he had enough time and money to indulge his curiosity. The only thing I could tell for sure was that he was lonely and didn't know what would make him feel complete.

At the airport, Don meets a young man who is wearing sunglasses and carrying a duffel bag identical to his. They look like they could be father and son. They pass each other with a brief nod. Don seems like he wants to speak to him, but he doesn't.

One of the women he visits, Dora, played by Frances Conroy, has become a real estate agent who lives with her husband, Ron, in a model of the prefabricated homes they sell. The décor is chilly and white with accents of pink roses.

"Shooter McGavin!" My brother and I exclaim when we see Christopher McDonald, who plays Ron onscreen.

Shooter McGavin was the villain from *Happy Gilmore* who famously tried to intimidate his rival, played by Adam Sandler, with the phrase "I eat pieces of shit like you for breakfast."

"You eat pieces of shit for breakfast?" Happy replies.

Outwitted, Shooter can only yell, "No!" before quickly walking away.

Happy Gilmore was one of our favorite movies growing up, and the actor who played Shooter showing up in the film eclipsed Don's bittersweet narrative and brought us back to a simpler time. It felt good to share something from my childhood that had nothing to do with who my real father was, nothing to do with my parents' denial or the fear I felt about what the next day with my family would bring.

Don visits three other women who also lead vastly different lives from what they had in the past. Don discovers that a fifth woman, the one he originally thought had written him the letter, died five years prior. He buys flowers to place on her grave.

While my mother and I were arguing that evening, one of the points she raised was that my biological father could be dead. I didn't know why she would say that, especially because she insisted she didn't know who he was. Was she trying to dissuade me from looking for him, or did she know something else?

In the end, Don returns to New Jersey, having not discovered the mother of his son or if he has a son at all. He has a bandage over his eye from getting punched in the face at the last home he visited.

Back home, he finds another pink envelope, identical to the first. The letter is signed this time, and it turns out to be from the ex-girlfriend who'd left him at the beginning of the film. She says she still has feelings for him.

He meets Winston to debrief him about the trip. Winston, an aspiring mystery writer, is excited, but Don is suspicious. Was the whole thing a hoax? Did his ex-girlfriend want to get back at him? Did Winston get in touch with Don's past lovers beforehand and send him on a wild goose chase? Was it a ploy to make Don consider having a family?

Outside the restaurant, Don spots the young man he saw at the airport at the start of the film. He is wearing a track jacket, black with red stripes, nearly identical to Don's.

Don offers to buy him lunch as "a guy who wants to buy another guy a sandwich." They eat outside, sitting on overturned milk crates, in the alley behind the restaurant. The young man says he is on a "sort-of" road trip. Don asks him about his interests, and he answers, "Philosophy."

After a moment, the young man asks, "As just a guy who gave another guy a sandwich, do you have, like, any philosophical tips or anything?"

Don pauses for a moment, then replies, "Well, the past is gone. I know that. The future isn't here yet, whatever it's going to be. So, all there is, is . . . is this. The present. That's it."

Don tells the young man he thinks he is his father, but he's taken the conversation too far, and the young man flees.

In the end Don never learns if the young man he met was his son, or if he has a son at all. His visits only show him that the women in his life have moved on; that what happened between them twenty years ago is in the distant past. Would that have changed if one of them were really the mother of his child? The film's plot was far-fetched, but its themes weren't. People reunited with their biological parents all the time. It was a natural instinct, wasn't it?

"We have to watch all the credits," I said as Pat shifted, ready to get up. It was late. We waited until almost all the credits rolled until we saw my friend's name.

"See!" I said, pointing to the screen. "The first name under In-terns: Tara Anderson! She said everyone on the production team got one of those black-and-red jackets."

We turned the TV off.

"This doesn't change anything," Pat said after a silence. "I mean, it changes everything, but not between us."

"Yeah," I said. "I know."

Nineteen

The next day, we woke up early and drove to New York City for the Macy's Thanksgiving Day Parade.

None of us wanted to be there, but my parents had planned it as part of the trip, and my mother insisted that we go.

"When I was little, I always wanted to go to the Macy's Thanksgiving Day Parade," she said. "But my parents never took us on any vacations."

As we walked through the cold streets filled with people and noise, I tried to ask my mother about the guys she knew in college. It was a small, rural school in western Pennsylvania.

"I mean, how many black guys could there have been?" I asked, my voice getting lost in the din. We fell behind my dad and brothers. It seemed like she wanted to talk to me.

"There were two I knew," she said.

"Did you date them?" I asked.

"One of them, Ed, worked in the dining hall with Karen and me on work study." Karen was one of the girls whose face I recognized in the photo. She and my mother grew up in the same town and were roommates in college.

"He was tall and shy," she said. "He wore glasses. He used to talk to me, and I was friendly with him. I didn't want him to think I didn't like him because he was black."

"Was it him?" I asked.

"I don't think so," my mother said. "We didn't hang out with him outside the cafeteria. I don't think he was at the party that night."

"What do you remember from that night?" I yelled, drowned out by the marching band.

"Nothing," she said.

Spider-Man and Mickey Mouse filled the sky. I wanted to find somewhere quiet to talk, but we had to keep moving, jostled forward by the throng of parade-goers in dark coats.

"What about the other guy?" I yelled. "How did you know him?"

"Isn't this great?" she said, looking up at the floats and tall buildings. "I wanted us to be able to see a Broadway musical while we were here, or a play. Don't you want to see a play?"

I didn't know whether she couldn't hear my question above the cheers and marching bands or was avoiding the subject, but from that moment on, we only talked about how nice New York City was and how much she'd wanted to come here as a kid.

For Thanksgiving, we always had a big turkey. My mother used Martha Stewart's technique of basting the turkey in butter and white wine and covering it with cheesecloth so it didn't burn. It always turned out delicious. My grandmother brought the traditional green bean casserole, made with Campbell's mushroom soup and topped with French's fried onions. Mashed potatoes, glazed sweet potatoes, cranberry sauce, and my personal favorites, gravy and stuffing, filled out the table. My mom made everything from scratch. My dad tore up the loaves of sliced white bread for the stuffing, which he dropped into a brown grocery bag. My mom then put it into a chafing dish with the other ingredients, covered it with tinfoil, and put it in the oven to roast. Because she was wary of us getting salmonella she didn't put any of the stuffing inside the turkey.

Dessert was also homemade: pumpkin pie, apple pie, cookies and biscotti, my grandmother's iced nut roll. My mother and grandmother were great cooks and bakers.

When my brothers and I were younger, my grandparents hosted Thanksgiving dinner. My mom's younger brother, Rob, and I didn't like mushrooms, so the stuffing never had mushrooms in it. If we found mushrooms in any of the dishes on the table, we would complain. Luckily, the mushrooms in the green bean casserole were undetectable, and I didn't learn until I was much older how it was made. By then, I was mature enough to accept it, but I still wouldn't eat mushrooms in anything else.

After we got a dining room set for our house on Ash Court, my mother started hosting Thanksgiving. By then, my uncle Rob was married to Lorie, and soon their three kids, in addition to my mother's parents, joined us. Liane, my mother's older sister, who was my favorite aunt when I was little, moved away years ago and did not keep in touch. Sometimes members of my father's family would make the journey from Philadelphia, but usually we celebrated with just my mother's side of the family.

We had leftovers for days. There were always fights; my mom would tell my dad he got a wrong ingredient at the store; my dad insisted that he got the thing she'd asked for, and the argument would continue until he went out to the store again. In the end, though, good food, family, and warmth prevailed.

When we got back to Princeton, the sun had already set. By the time we realized we needed to do something for Thanksgiving dinner, all the restaurants in the area were closed. We ended up going to the Wawa convenience store near campus and getting frozen Stouffer's pizzas and Hungry-Man meatloaf dinners to heat up in the hotel room's microwave. The harsh fluorescent lights made our faces look even more haggard, the tension between us more edged. I avoided making eye contact with the cashier, a young dark-skinned man, possibly Indian, as he rang up the purchases my father paid for. I wondered what he thought of this adult family coming in to buy microwaveable food on Thanksgiving when the only other customers were a few college students. Did he wonder why I, an African American, was with them?

When we returned to the Marriott, we took turns microwaving our frozen dinners in exhausted silence. We ate with plastic forks and poured our twenty-ounce bottles of soda from the hotel vending machine into paper cups. The french bread pizza I'd gotten was still frozen in the middle, but I didn't bother reheating it. I just sat on the couch and crunched through the cold, tomato-y dough.

My mind flashed back to the meeting with my therapist and her comment that I looked so much darker to her after she learned I was African American. After the shock of the session wore off, I wondered how she saw me before I revealed my race. Did she have a definite idea about my ethnicity, or did she think of me as vaguely brown or simply nonwhite? Growing up, people of other ethnicities would often ask me if I was what they were. Was I Indian? Jewish? Arab? I'd politely answer no, and I couldn't help feeling as though I'd disappointed them. I didn't know enough back then to answer that my mother was Italian and my father was black. Would that have changed how they saw me? It occurred to me that even other nonwhite people draw a line between black and brown, but I wasn't sure where the line was drawn or on which side of that line I fell.

Twenty

Before my parents left Princeton the next day, we decided that, before we went any further with the discussion of my biological father, we should be absolutely sure of my paternity. The next time I would be home was Christmas break, so my mom said she would order a paternity test, and my dad and I could provide our DNA samples then.

"We can do it if you think it's really necessary," my mother said with exasperation as I agreed, perhaps too enthusiastically. It seemed that, deep down, she believed the test would prove that my dad was indeed my real father and that, once again, I was making a big fuss over nothing. I knew she wanted the specter of this strange man who had entered our family's life, brought racially charged conflict, and stirred up old trauma for her, out of our life for good. In her mind, a DNA test would provide a medically conclusive end to the conversation.

My father quietly assented as if he, too, thought the paternity test might be just a formality and that the truth had been there all along.

"We're doing this for you, Bean," he said. "No matter what the result is, it won't change anything. You'll always be my princess."

As he spoke, his voice was more affectionate but less sure than my mother's.

It felt like there was much more riding on the outcome of a paternity test for me than there was for my parents. They had made their choices in life, but this one big choice had been made for me. Their identities weren't in question. My mother knew she was my biological mother, and my father had already been my dad for nearly twenty-eight years. When my mother was pregnant, he made the decision to marry her and decided the child she carried was his. She decided to keep the child, and after having me, they decided to have two more children. My parents decided—perhaps tacitly—to never talk about my race and raise me as white.

I was not taught what it meant to be a biracial African American in a white family, or rather, I never got to decide with my family what that would mean for me and for us. Even though my mother's revelation wasn't what I wanted or expected to hear, I thought that maybe now I would at least get to choose how I identified in the world. Given the events my mother described, it seemed like my biological father was not someone I would like to get to know, but at least now I would be able to make that choice for myself rather than having the information withheld. My parents would still be my parents; my brothers would still be my brothers. We would still have all the memories of family vacations to the Jersey Shore, all the first days of school, all the birthdays, Mother's Days, Father's Days, and other days that had been special. But a test showing that I was not my father's biological daughter meant that there was a reason for why I looked the way I looked, a reason why my high school friends had joked about Jerome the milkman, a reason why I always felt like some part of me was missing. It would place my whole personal, social, and family life in a different light.

"We wouldn't be having this conversation if he had been white," my mother said during our argument. She was right. If *he* had been white, I may have never known I had a different father than my brothers. But if my conception had been as my mother described it, would she even know? If her assailant had been white, how would she have known I wasn't my dad's child when I was born? There may have been no secret to keep—unless she knew more about the person than she let on.

My parents and brother drove off, and once again I was alone on campus. I drove back to my place through quiet streets. Because it was still Thanksgiving break, most people on campus were with their families. My roommate was staying with her husband at the University of Pennsylvania, where he was a graduate student. The house was empty.

In the silence, I thought about everything that had happened and how I felt about taking a paternity test. Did I want the test to prove my dad was my biological father? No, I didn't. As much as I loved my dad, I felt there was no going back from the conversation I'd had with my family. Unlike my parents, who hoped the test would disprove their fears and close the Pandora's box that had been opened, I wanted to know the truth and move forward. Deep down, I knew the test would confirm their fears and my hopes, but I knew that no matter what the test said, my dad would always be my dad.

The uncomfortable question was how I would feel when the test confirmed that my biological father was also my mother's rapist. I didn't even want to think about that. I wanted to know there was someone out there connected to me, who would welcome me as part of his family and provide me with a key to my African American lineage. I wanted to know there was someone out there who was tall, good-looking, athletic, left-handed, and artistic like me, whom

I could look to and see resemblances in physique and character and who would allow me to feel more confident in my identity; who would help me feel legitimate.

But even as I wished for these things, I knew it was a fantasy. In reality, my mom didn't remember or didn't want to remember the man who'd impregnated her. He could be a deadbeat, a bad guy. Someone who didn't remember her, a girl he took advantage of one drunken college night nearly thirty years ago. Who would want to remember that? My heart sank. There was no silver lining to this cloud.

To say that my biological father was a black man who'd raped my mother sounded like the most horrible racist cliché. It spoke of the warning slave owners intoned about the need to keep the sexually ravenous black men away from the good, pure white women. I was still learning about black history, but I knew about Emmett Till, who, at fourteen, had been beaten to death for allegedly harassing a white woman. I knew there was a whole mythology of black rapists targeting white women, when in fact most sexual assault takes place between people of the same race. Interracial rape was rare, but not impossible. I felt torn between my newly discovered blackness and my—and my mother's—gender. Was I supposed to feel more sympathy for the black man or the white woman? It felt like I had to choose. By telling me her story, my mother drew another line, and I would have to decide where I stood. If I believed her, I would have to disavow my biological father, whoever he was; if I decided to look for him, I would be betraying her. I didn't think things had to be this way, but those were her feelings. Once again, I didn't feel like I had a choice.

Was it naïve of me to wonder if a black male student surrounded by white peers on a campus in rural Pennsylvania in the 1970s would take the risk of even being alone with a white girl in a questionable situation? Would a black college student not consider the political ramifications of that kind of act? The '70s were a time of feminism and civil rights on college campuses, but maybe not at the small rural college my mother attended. Maybe drunk college students were just drunk college students and didn't make good decisions, no matter the race or the decade. Maybe, at a house party with so many substances being consumed, no one cared who was hanging out with whom.

Or were these just excuses? It felt dangerous to speculate.

"There was no one I could tell," my mother said when we were in New York. "Back then, no one took it seriously. You weren't a victim—you were a sucker. You were asking for it. I wasn't even sure what happened. Who was I going to tell?"

Twenty-one

Like Thanksgiving, Christmas at my parents' house was always a big event. Every year, my parents hosted a Christmas Eve party for our closest friends, and the house would be filled with guests, good food, laughter, decorations, twinkling lights, and a decked-out Christmas tree in the front window.

Each family had kids the ages of me and my brothers. Most of them were friends from school and, for my brothers, football. It made for a houseful of twenty or so. We served hors d'oeuvres on the island in the center of the kitchen. My dad took great pride in his task of boiling and chilling the basinful of jumbo shrimp for our version of shrimp cocktail, which was the centerpiece. Around it, there were plates of crackers and cheese, nuts, fruit and vegetable plates, and other dishes brought by our guests.

Dinner was served buffet-style in the dining room: a whole glazed ham, a turkey, both of which were sliced on a platter for convenient sandwiches; a classic Italian American dish like stuffed shells or chicken parmesan, soft dinner rolls, more cheese, and a bevy of side dishes. Most guests brought plates of cookies, which they set next to pumpkin pie and my grandmother's traditional nut and poppy seed rolls. My mother always made sugar cookies, which we as kids always helped decorate, and a gingerbread house for the center of the dessert table.

Christmas Eve was one of the few nights during the year when my parents drank wine or mixed drinks, which made them merrier but less watchful than usual, and when we were in high school we would use this opportunity to sneak a bottle or two away into the basement while the adults enjoyed themselves upstairs.

Our least favorite part of the evening was the family photograph. The moms and dads wore Christmas sweaters, while the rest of us were made to wear Christmas colors or at the very least dress up; for me, a pretty skirt and blouse, and for my brothers, corduroy pants, collared shirts, and plaid ties. Each family would take turns having their photo taken, usually a few times, in front of our festively decorated fireplace hung with embroidered stockings and surrounded by red poinsettias, flickering candles, and statues of Santa Claus.

Even with the family photo looming, I always looked forward to our Christmas Eve parties. It was a time when my mother smiled, her cheeks rosy from wine, and all the arguing throughout the day that had led up to the event ceased. My parents were gracious hosts among their friends. They were at their best and were happy.

As my younger brothers and I got older, first graduating from high school, then college, the Christmas Eve parties became smaller, quieter. Fewer families came by. Some stopped by only for a short time, for the sake of tradition, to wish us a merry Christmas and to drop off some cookies before visiting other friends or family. Still, we cooked a lot of food. We went to mass on Christmas Day and came downstairs Christmas morning to a pile of presents under the tree. Eventually, the gatherings became just a few good family friends and a chance to see my girlfriends from high school.

This year, my parents decided before they left Princeton that there would be no party. This year when I came home for Christmas, my father and I would be taking a paternity test. It didn't seem like the right time to celebrate with friends.

When I flew into Pittsburgh, my dad picked me up from the airport. We were mostly silent on the long ride from the airport to Wexford. I was always amused and touched by the three statues that greeted me as I arrived at the Pittsburgh International Airport: a young, brown-haired George Washington in his blue-and-red lieutenant colonel's uniform; a scaled-down replica of a *Tyrannosaurus rex* skeleton rearing up on its hind legs; and Franco Harris in his Steelers' uniform and helmet, leaning down with a football in his hands, balanced on one leg, catching the Immaculate Reception.

George Washington was part of Pittsburgh's history because he helped the British take Fort Duquesne from the French during the Seven Years' War in 1758. On that site, the British would later build Fort Pitt.

The *T. rex* skeleton represented the life-sized one that formed the crowning exhibit at the Carnegie Museum of Natural History. I was awed at seeing the forty-foot skeleton as a child on a class field trip to the museum. It stood like a skeletal Godzilla, with its menacing jaws open and clawed hands ready to strike. The *T. rex* became the museum's calling card and a symbol of Pittsburgh's cultural importance.

The Immaculate Reception was one of the most legendary plays in the history of football, with Franco Harris scooping up a botched pass and running it for a touchdown to bring the Steelers a playoff victory. The game took place at Three Rivers Stadium in Pittsburgh against the Oakland Raiders just two days before Christmas in 1972. It must have seemed like a Christmas miracle. Growing up, it felt like the Steelers were part of the pantheon of saints, so it was fitting that Myron Cope, our famous sports announcer, named the play after the Catholic Church's most sacred event, the Virgin Mary's Immaculate Conception of Jesus Christ. To me, the statue of Franco Harris catching the Immaculate Reception symbolized all the pieces of my childhood rolled into one.

When I was younger, I thought people were saying *Frank O'Harris*, and never having seen the player, I assumed he was Irish. When I was a teenager, my mother and I were eating at an Italian restaurant in the mall after what must have been for her an exhausting afternoon of shopping. A large, dark-featured man sat at a table in front of us.

"That's Franco Harris," my mother said and motioned toward the man. Later, I learned that Harris was Italian and African American.

Those three figures, which I had seen upon my arrivals to Pittsburgh for years, seemed like a Holy Trinity of sorts and summed up Pittsburgh and its values better than any words of welcome ever could.

As we drove north, I watched the city give way, as it always did on this drive, to rolling hills covered with bare trees and a wide, gray sky. It was getting dark, and by the time we reached Wexford, the Christmas lights on the houses in our cul-de-sac shone through the dark, along with illuminated, inflated candy canes, Santa on his sleigh pulled by all eight reindeer, and a family of giant inflated snowmen. There was a dusting of snow on the ground, but it wasn't snowing. Things felt surreal, as if I were experiencing them from far away. Home was familiar and alien at the same time. I was both comforted and irritated by the displays of holiday cheer I saw on Ash Court, as if everything in the world were fine and there was no cause for outrage. It was a suburban cocoon, and I wondered if any of its residents, including my parents, cared about the world outside. It wasn't fair: I didn't know the other families on our street or how they lived, but the place had become symbolic. It represented my own ignorance, a place where we could hide and push the rest of the world away.

As we pulled up the steep driveway to our house, I could see the white lights of our Christmas tree twinkling in the front window and the colored lights on the trees and shrubs in our front yard. When the groaning garage door sounded, so did Bailey's barking. Bailey was a golden retriever husky mix my parents got after Knight passed away. She was sweeter and less bold, though just as poorly trained. She knew Dad was coming home. The flight wasn't long, but my limbs felt stiff and numb as I got out of the car, climbed the steps, and opened the door to the kitchen.

Bailey accosted me right away, jumping, licking, barking; even though I hadn't been home in a while, she remembered my scent. The house was still decorated warmly and festively as usual, all my mother's Santas and holiday keepsakes on display. Cinnamon-scented candles still burned in the kitchen; my mother was rolling out dough on the counter. She turned from the sink and came to give me a hug. We pushed the big, excited dog aside and embraced just as my dad came in from the garage carrying my bag. I didn't see his face in that moment, but I had a feeling he was relieved to see me hug my mom. In a way, I was relieved, too.

"Everything looks great!" I exclaimed as the sights and sounds brought back memories. There were carols playing on the radio; the stockings hung over the fireplace; and a gas-lit fire flickered in the hearth. "What are you baking?" I asked.

"Oh, the usual," my mom said, returning to the counter. "Grandma Mary and Granddad will be coming over on Christmas Day. Rob and Lorie and the kids might come, too." Her tone was flat, attempting cheerfulness. I wanted to ask if they'd gotten the DNA tests, but I knew the time wasn't right. I watched her back and bowed head working dough on the counter for a piecrust.

"Want any help?" I ventured, though the last thing I wanted was to stand in the kitchen alongside my mother pretending this was a holiday like any other.

"That's okay," she replied. "I'm almost done anyway."

"Okay," I said. "I'm going upstairs—need to catch up on sleep. Good night." I was relieved as I walked up the stairs, but still felt trepidation about what the next few days would bring. My dad had taken my bag up to my room and had quietly gone to sleep. The house felt cold and it kept me on edge.

As I layered myself in sweatshirts and sweatpants, I tried to settle into my youngest brother's old bedroom, which now served as the guest room. The heavy oak furniture, the quilted bedspread, and radio on the nightstand brought me back to an earlier time. There were high school sports photos of my brothers and me in the bookcase; me, in my team uniform, down on one knee holding a basketball at my side, the other hand on my hip, with my puffy hair pulled partway back, falling in triangles above my shoulders. It was hard to look at these photos, which seemed like they were from another life. My brothers were no longer the football and baseball stars that lived in these photos, and I was no longer the varsity athlete that made my parents so proud.

The next day, the morning of Christmas Eve, my father and I did the DNA tests. I swabbed the inside of my cheek hard, until it hurt, to make sure they got enough skin cells to analyze the sample. We paid for expedited service so that we'd get the test results in a few weeks rather than a few months. A lot was riding on those spitty cotton swabs. My dad drove the tests to the post office, making an awkward joke about not wanting them to get lost in the mail. My brothers arrived later in the day, and my dad picked them both up at the airport. He would never consider us taking a taxi or getting a ride from someone else.

"I'll meet you in the usual place," he'd say, which was just beyond George Washington and Franco Harris.

After going to the post office, my dad came home with Chinese takeout for dinner. It was Christmas Eve, and we all felt the disparity between the current meal and our traditional repast.

"At least it's not the Wawa," my father said, trying to inject some levity into the apprehensive room. No one laughed.

In the weeks following Thanksgiving, my mother and I had countless arguments over the phone. They always ended with her saying that she wished she'd never told me in the first place. For her, it was all in the past. But her past was my present.

I felt immature and ungrateful—two words she often used—for insisting we talk about the forbidden subject. I wanted to know who my father was, no matter the circumstances. I knew it hurt my mother, but I wasn't able to sweep the subject under the rug like she did. It meant too much to me. Wasn't it something I had a right to know?

"I don't know a lot about my own father," my mom would retort. "I barely know any of my relatives. They don't care about me!"

"Mom, that's not the same. You know where you come from. You've had your father your whole life."

"So have you." It was true. I grew up with a loving, devoted father who called me his princess and bent over backward to make me happy.

And yet.

What I couldn't articulate then was that the condition of my whole upbringing had been an insidious lie; that to be part of my loving family, I had to tacitly agree to pass for white. I thought about sitting in the car with my dad after high school basketball practice when he'd told me it would be dishonest of me to apply for minority scholarships and not to mention it to my mother. Looking back, I couldn't tell if he honestly believed I was white or if he was just steering me away from a dangerous subject. If he really believed I was white, why would he tell me not to mention the subject to my mother? My heart sank to think they were both in on the lie, both colluding to keep the subject of race—my race—out of our lives.

So that was the agreement—to not ask questions, to avoid and deflect the queries of friends, acquaintances, and strangers. If I openly identified as African American, I was the one being dishonest.

Now that the truth had come out and I realized that people outside my family were correct in their assumptions about my identity, I felt like my parents were asking me to avoid the subject for their sake, not mine. To my mom, my biological father wasn't a real person. When I referred to him as my biological father, she snapped, "Don't call him that! That's not a father!"

When she did refer to him directly, which was seldom, she called him "the donor."

Weeks passed, then months.

We asked my mother if she had gotten the results of the paternity test. She said no, they'd never sent them.

More weeks passed, and we waited.

I came home for spring break. We asked her again. She said that she'd lost the password and could not access the results online.

Finally, my father took a stand—something that rarely happened—and made her give us the results. In the months since Christmas, my father had taken a job that relocated him to Scranton, Pennsylvania, which was close to Princeton but about three hundred miles from Pittsburgh. My mother worked as a nurse and did not want to give up her job at the hospital, so she stayed in Wexford with the rambunctious Bailey and the reclusive cat, Tilly. My parents never spoke of my father's relocation as a separation; it was strictly for his job. From what I could tell, the mood between them had changed. My father was used to commuting and traveling for work, and he usually flew home to Pittsburgh on the weekends. The arrangement didn't seem out of the ordinary, and we all went to Scranton to see my dad's one-bedroom apartment filled with rented furniture. We made jokes about Scranton and *The Office,* but ever so carefully, my father was creating space between himself and my mother.

My mother revealed that the results from the DNA test had been in her desk the whole time; she just hadn't wanted to face them.

My dad read them first.

They proved what my parents had been so unwilling to admit for all these years: my father and I were not biologically related.

By this point, the verdict was not surprising at all, and yet, at the same time, I was surprised. It was the first piece of indisputable, scientific evidence that I was another man's child. My looks on their own had never been enough for my parents to admit the truth. They liked to point out that my dad's skin was darker than mine, and that I was trying to manufacture or exaggerate my difference. I wondered if the test results would change their minds. I was shocked and elated and devastated and heartbroken and hopeful and curious all at the same time.

Even though, to the outside world, my appearance alone was enough to signal that I was black, half-black, or a person of color, in my family, that part of me always felt invisible. The part of me that spoke of difference, even though it was staring them in the face every day, was not enough to convince my family that there was something we needed to address. Their dismissal made me feel like I was not enough, that there was something inadequate about my looks that didn't properly signal race or ethnicity like everyone else's. I experienced what I would describe as racial dysphoria. I never felt black enough for references to my race to seem any more than an uncomfortable joke, and, despite my parents' insistence, I wasn't white enough to blend in with those around me. Growing up, I wanted my skin to be darker so that I wouldn't look so ambiguous and so my family couldn't just ignore that part of who I was. In high school I used tan foundation, and my mother would say, "That's too dark for you," and give me a tone that made my cheeks chalky and pink.

Now was the time for the conversation I'd been waiting for. Since we had established that my dad was not my biological father, my question—the logical question—was: *Who is?*

My dad had discreetly left my mom and me alone in the backyard to talk. It was the first hint of spring. My mom filled the silence between us by giving me a tour of her garden, pointing out the plants that were coming back and those she'd need to replant. We were standing beneath the pergola covered in bare wisteria vines when I asked her, "So who is my real father?"

"Don't call him that!" she snapped, then added, "I do not have that information."

"How is that possible?" I asked. "How could you not know?"

She recounted the story she'd told me during our first conversation on the topic. "I was at a party, I drank too much . . ."

"Wait," I said. "I thought you said you were drugged, that someone put something in your drink?"

"Well, maybe I was," she said noncommittally. "I woke up the next morning in my dorm room. I don't know how I got home; I don't remember anything about that night."

Three weeks old, with my parents on my first visit to my grandparents' house. Beaver, Pennsylvania, 1977. (COURTESY OF MARY MARTIN)

My dad teaches me to ride a bike. Flourtown, Pennsylvania, 1979. (COURTESY OF THE AUTHOR)

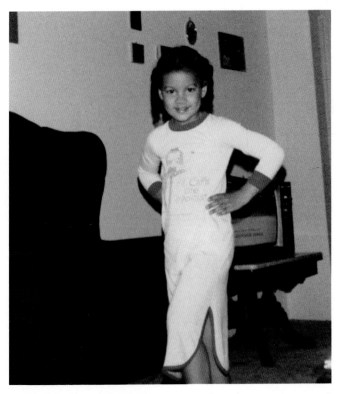

Four years old. My nightshirt says, "All Girls Are Important."
Harrisburg, Pennsylvania, 1982. (COURTESY OF THE AUTHOR)

Christmas-sweater photo with my brothers, Patrick and Thomas. Wexford, Pennsylvania, 1995. (COURTESY OF THE AUTHOR)

With my brothers after my dissertation defense. Princeton, New Jersey, 2007. (COURTESY OF THE AUTHOR)

With my former in-laws for an Igbo memorial celebration. London, United Kingdom, 2011.

With my aunt, Kathleen Dunn (my father's sister), and my newborn nephew, Harrison Dunn. Wexford, Pennsylvania, 2015. (COURTESY OF THE AUTHOR)

My maternal grandfather in his U.S. Army uniform during the Korean War, approximately 1950. His family emigrated to the U.S. from Italy around 1920.

My maternal great-great-grandparents, Martin Zelenak and Anna Potochnak Zelenak, and their family. They were born in Austria-Hungary in the early 1880s and emigrated to the U.S. between 1905–1910. My great-grandmother, Anna Zelenak, is topmost. Beaver, Pennsylvania, around 1920.

Portrait of my maternal great-great grandmother (*center row, second from right*), my great aunt (*center row, third from right*), my great uncle (*center row, far right*), and their children. My great uncle was a Greek Orthodox priest and the brother of my great grandfather, Michael Mikedis. Michael Mikedis was born in Chios, Greece in 1895 and emigrated to the United States on his own in the 1920s. According to my grandmother, my great uncle's family never visited the U.S., but they must have sent this photo, taken in Chios, Greece, around 1940.

"Then how do you know you were raped?" I asked.

"I don't," she said. "Maybe I wasn't. I don't know."

"I don't understand," I said, trying to wrap my mind around what she was telling me. We sat down on cushioned lawn chairs. "Wait, are you telling me now that you were not . . . you know?"

"I'm sorry, Sarah. I wish I could tell you what you want to know, but I can't."

None of it made sense. Why would she tell me my biological father had raped her unless she had been sure? Why would she say that she was drugged if it weren't true? I pressed, but she wouldn't say anything more. It seemed as if she were trying to protect someone. She had flown off the handle over Thanksgiving when my dad had suggested it was one of the guys she knew in college. If she wasn't protecting the biological father, then was she protecting my dad from having to confront the man whose child he'd raised? Mostly, it seemed like she was protecting herself. Maybe she was protecting me, too. All I felt when I brought up the subject was hostility, not compassion, so I couldn't understand what she went through then or what she was going through now.

In movies and on television, big family dramas are resolved before the credits roll. A secret is revealed, people are hurt, relationships fall apart, and then one or both parties realize it's better to forgive and forget than hold on to bad feelings. There's a tearful reunion, everyone is happy and reconciled, and life goes on as before.

This is not what happened for my mother and me. Every conversation we had afterward ended the same way—in yelling, tears, my demanding that she tell the truth, and her saying she didn't know or couldn't remember.

I felt betrayed because in the days that followed her revelation, unsure of what to do or where to turn, I'd called a rape crisis hotline.

"My mother was raped twenty-seven years ago," I said unsteadily when a volunteer answered. "What should I do? Is there anything I can do, legally?"

The volunteer talked to me about the statute of limitations for rape, that in some states, like New Jersey, there was no set period of time after which a victim of rape could not come forward. In Pennsylvania, the statute of limitation was twelve years. I thought of myself at twelve, how each year of my life after that was another year my mother's assailant could not be brought to justice. All I'd felt was anger toward whoever harmed my mother; I wanted revenge. I didn't think it was fair that there was a rapist out there who took advantage of my mother and was leading a normal life. He had to be brought to justice. If my mother didn't want to pursue legal action or couldn't do so under the law, then I was determined to do it for her. In those early days, the only reason I wanted to find my biological father was to put him in prison.

In my second year of grad school, I went to Prague for a summer language course. While I was there, the Vltava River flooded and a state of emergency was declared in the city. Classes were canceled, and we, the foreign students, were instructed to stay in the dormitory. Naturally, we used this as an excuse to party and get blackout drunk.

During the summer program, I had become friends with and subsequently dated two guys. One was Kami, an American who was half-Czech and half-Sudanese. Though he identified as black, he looked Mexican and often told us how Spanish-speaking folks in New York City, where he lived, would disapprove of him not knowing "his language." The other was Felix, who was German.

On the day of the flood party, I wasn't dating either one of them. We drank vodka straight from the bottle as sirens blared in the streets. We joked about a Soviet invasion. It was the middle of the day, not even close to night. Eventually, when I was so drunk I could hardly stand, I groped my way from the common room to a bedroom to lie down.

I must have passed out immediately, because when I woke up some time later, it was still daylight. My head was foggy, and my hips were incredibly sore. I looked on the floor next to the bed and saw a used condom; someone had had sex with me. At least they'd used protection; that was my first thought. Felix was lying on the bed across the room reading. He was fully clothed and gave no indication that anything had happened between us or that he'd seen anything happen. My panties were on, but the cargo skirt I was wearing was scrunched around my waist. *So,* I thought, *did I have sex and simply not remember? Who was it with? Could I have been conscious enough to put my underwear back on if I couldn't even remember anyone getting into bed with me?*

In the other room, the party continued, and no one noticed my absence. I didn't see Kami, and more important, I was too embarrassed to ask where he was. If I found him, would I have said, "Hey, did you—or someone else—have sex with me? You'll have to tell me, because I don't remember." The idea mortified me. I felt stupid for putting myself in the situation by getting so drunk that I'd passed out. It never crossed my mind that my being assaulted was someone else's fault.

My attention returned to my sore hips and pelvis. I'd never been that sore from sex, not that I could remember. Then a terrible thought: What if it had been more than one person? There were many male students in the program, but none of which I thought would have had the temerity to do that to me while I was unconscious. The word *rape* didn't even crystalize in my mind at the time because, I reasoned, since I had been involved with both Kami and Felix in the past, if it had been either of them, I might have consented if I were conscious. But I hadn't wanted to have sex at that time. I'd gone into the bedroom to lie down and get some rest. I was alone when I went into the room and had intended to stay that way. My head was still spinning. Without a word, I pulled my skirt down, smoothed it, got out of bed, stepped over the used condom, and went to rejoin the group as if nothing had happened.

Twenty-two

I now found myself in the worst possible scenario: I felt my mother was lying to me. When it happened to me, I had been on birth control, and the assailant had used a condom. Since I was passed out, there was no way for me to know whether the person had been black or white or anything else about his identity. The only way I would have known (assuming the assailant did not confess the liaison to me, which he did not) was if I would have had a child. Since the prospective men were of different races, the child would have provided a clue.

In my mother's case, it seemed that, if things had happened to her in the same way they'd happened to me, then she could only have known her assailant was black because I was. If that were truly the case, she was lying about not realizing I was of mixed race from the beginning. And if she realized I was black from the beginning, she must have had some idea, as I had, who the potential assailant was. Even though I was passed out during the act and heavily intoxicated beforehand, I still remembered, at least vaguely, what had happened at the party before and after. She seemed to have had a complete memory wipe not only of that night but of everything that had happened that year in college before she went on spring break with my dad. She couldn't remember the encounter itself, couldn't remember what happened afterward, and had no clue who might have been with her.

From my own experience, I knew how embarrassing and humiliating it was to be in that situation. When I woke up, I had so many questions.

I thought back to the scene in the movie *Kids,* where Jennie is passed out on the couch, fully clothed, and her male friend approaches her for sex. "Jennie, wake up," he says softly as he kisses her, touches her breasts, and massages her stomach. She rolls over, half shooing him away, but shows no sign of waking up. He is horny and persists. He takes her jeans and panties off, maneuvering her lifeless limbs.

"Don't worry, Jennie, it's me, Casper," he says as he fucks her unresponsive body.

He is on top of her for what seems like a long time; her legs are draped over his shoulders, her knees level with her ears.

It must have been the same position I was in for my hips and pelvis to have been so sore. How else could you fuck a girl who was passed out cold? Everyone around them is passed out, too, so there were no witnesses. Did he put her pants back on afterward? I doubt it. He doesn't use protection, either.

At the end of the film, he wakes up on the same couch (Jennie is nowhere in sight) and says, "Jesus Christ, what happened?" He seems to have no memory of what happened, either, or else is simply in disbelief at his and his friends' levels of debauchery.

I also thought about the night in college I spent with Craig after the Barenaked Ladies concert. When Craig passed out, I didn't violate him or continue to have any sexual contact with him. I left him as he was and went to bed without touching him further. In the morning, when he was still too drunk to walk, Tara and I helped dress him, walked him to the car, and drove him home. I didn't take advantage of his vulnerable state. I didn't even consider it. Why would I? The same thing happened with a guy I met on spring break in college. He was drunker than I was, and not long after we went back to my hotel room, he passed out on the bed. I immediately stopped kissing him, got up, and waited for our friends to come back to the room so they could take him back to his place. It would not have been moral or enjoyable to continue intimacy with him. How could someone look at their romantic partner passed out and think otherwise? Someone who looks at a passed-out person and sees a sexual opportunity is a predator, not a friend. In that situation, no matter how drunk the victim is, he or she is not to blame. I didn't think Craig or the guy I met on spring break counted themselves lucky because they didn't get taken advantage of while they were passed out; the possibility probably never even crossed their minds.

So why did I only blame myself for what happened to me and blame my mother for not knowing what happened to her?

After the flood, we went back to our classes, and I never spoke about what happened. I had the same friends as before, and as far as I knew, no one whispered about what had happened at the party. I put it out of my mind as the activities of the summer continued— seeing Czech-language films, practicing my broken German with some of the German students, acting as an English interpreter on our walking tours, and helping clean up the destruction wrought by the flood around the city. There was too much to do to think about that strange encounter. Like my mom, I kept the confusing, humiliating event to myself.

As I sat in my parents' backyard talking to my mother, I still couldn't see her point of view.

"What's hard for me to understand, Mom, is that, if you were willing to carry me and raise me—and you knew where I came from—why couldn't you just accept me for who I was instead of raising me as white? Why was that necessary?"

"I only saw you," she said. "I don't know how else to explain it to you."

I could see she was tired of talking about it and was frustrated because she thought what she was saying was self-explanatory. I'd never had a child and didn't know what it was like to have a new, vulnerable life in my care. Maybe the all-encompassing maternal feeling she described was something I couldn't comprehend. But a nagging skepticism returned. Surely not all mothers who had mixed-race children kept the child's identity and the identity of the father a secret.

My point of view felt just as self-explanatory to me. Why did I have to explain that in the world in which we live, it's important for a mixed-race, African American person to know their identity and understand where they come from? It's important for anyone to know. I knew that there was emotional trauma behind the explanation, and she had told me that she didn't know how to explain the situation to a child. She said she never wanted me to feel bad about who I was, and I guess for her, admitting my blackness was inextricably linked with the possibility of my feeling bad, knowing I came from an unwanted, hurtful event. She insisted, though, that things would have been different if the perpetrator had been white.

Twenty-three

I was born on December 6, 1977, at Chestnut Hill Hospital in Phila-delphia, Pennsylvania. Back then, we lived with my dad's folks at their house on Grove Avenue in Flourtown, Pennsylvania. I can look through family albums and see photos of my dad holding me right after I was born, looking down at me with excitement and a little be-wilderment, wearing a pair of turquoise scrubs the hospital gave him. When I was little, he wore those scrubs around the house until I was ten or eleven, at which point they got so faded and holey my mom made him throw them out. There's another shot of the three of us lying on a floral comforter in the room we shared in the Grove Avenue house, heads toward the camera, my mom's hair long, dark, and wavy, my dad's straight and black, mine short and curly.

My dad was completing his undergraduate degree at West Vir-ginia University. My mother had already left her college, and when I turned one we moved to an apartment in Morgantown, West Virginia, so that my dad could complete his studies. A year later we moved to State College because my dad was accepted into Pennsyl-vania State University's graduate program for public administration.

My first memories are of living in State College, running over to our neighbor's apartment, opening the door without being invited and breaking my friend's crayons. I was having a great time, but my mom had to explain to me that none of these behaviors were socially acceptable. I also remember the blue-and-white checked blanket that represented Penn State's colors; from a very young age I knew to root for the Nittany Lions.

My parents have told me about many of my antics during their college days: I would hide in the clothes racks or run away, inevitably to the toy section, while they were shopping. Once, a kindly stranger had to bring me to the security booth in the mall because she had found me, a two-year-old, roaming free. My parents were glad I returned safely. After getting over the shock and scare of my being lost, they laughed about these times. My mother told me that once, during a tantrum, I lay down in the middle of the street and she was laughing so hard she couldn't pick me up.

Back in Flourtown, where I attended preschool, my dad worked construction while he tried to parlay his MPA into a career. In the meantime, my mom worked at McDonald's. My dad and I dropped her off every day in a little rust-colored Volkswagen Beetle, and my treat was a pancake breakfast with sausage and lots of syrup. Some kids found Ronald McDonald creepy, but to me, he, Grimace, the Hamburglar, Birdie, and the Fry Guys were celebrities. I had a Ronald McDonald doll and figures of the characters from Happy Meals. As far as my four-year-old self was concerned, McDonald's was perfection.

I loved the house on Grove Avenue: the creaky staircase, the smell of my grandmother's coffee and cigarettes, the pantry at the top of the basement stairs with narrow shelves filled with cans and boxes of food that reached to the ceiling. I would chase my grandparents' cat,

Rosie, down those stairs and into the basement, a dark, mysterious world of old box fans, furniture, and card tables stacked with boxes of Christmas decorations. My dad's younger siblings, John and Kathleen, were aged twelve and nine at the time, and although they were my uncle and aunt, I saw them more as my big brother and sister. Because my grandmother was often ill, my mom took care of John and Kathleen too, making them lunch and getting them ready for school. I loved Uncle John and Aunt Kathleen, as I called them; I thought everything they did was cool. My dad's brother Steven was only one year younger than he, and by the time we moved back in, twenty-two-year-old Steven was already out of the house. I loved my uncle Stevie, who looked so much like my dad, though I rarely saw him.

My early years were very happy ones. When I was young, I never realized I was different because my family never made me feel that way. When I look at photos from those times now, as happy as they are, I can't understand how my parents and grandparents avoided the subject of my race; I looked so obviously different. But they loved me just as I was and didn't need any more explanation than that.

Even though the house on Grove Avenue was a fun and loving place when I lived there, my father's own childhood was fraught.

He grew up in Olney, a neighborhood in north Philadelphia, in the late 1950s and early 1960s. As the family grew and the demographics of the formerly redlined neighborhood changed, his family moved to Flourtown in Springfield County, a mostly Irish and Jewish suburb. His mother and her two younger sisters grew up at the Scotland School in Franklin County for orphaned and abandoned children of military veterans. My grandmother was valedictorian of her nursing program and had begun a promising career as a nurse when she was introduced to my grandfather, a handsome paratrooper from the Korean War. When they married and had children, at my grandfather's insistence she gave up her career. Later, my father would tell me that the illness she experienced for much of my childhood was depression. While my grandmother stayed home with the children and became increasingly depressed, my grandfather had extramarital affairs. My dad told me stories of his father staying away for days and weeks at a time and never knowing when he was going to be back. Eventually, a friend of his dad's from the Black Horse Pub would come by and say he saw Bob (my dad's father) with some woman and that he should be coming home soon. My dad's need for self-reliance at an early age helped him develop a strong and independent character, but he was also perpetually anxious and uncertain about the commitment of those he loved. He had a need for stability and a need to be needed. When my mother was younger, she was not particularly close to her parents, older sister, or younger brother. Even though our situation wasn't perfect, my parents both enjoyed the closeness and stability of having their own little family; in some ways it made up for their dysfunctional childhoods. I felt secure having young, energetic, and loving parents. Unlike my dad, I never feared one of my parents would walk out on me or not be there in the morning when I woke up.

My grandfather was home more regularly when we moved in, and he and my mother became friends. He liked to talk—to bullshit, as my grandfather put it—unlike her stern, distant father. In a way, he became the father she never had.

I was four years old when my brother Patrick was born on July 10, 1982, and by then, we had moved out of my grandparents' house to an apartment in Harrisburg, Pennsylvania. I was too young for preschool, and we only had one car, which my dad drove to work. My mom stayed home with me while my dad worked at a consulting job that would let him use his degree. My time in Harrisburg was a happy time, too. My best friends were twin boys who lived at the end of the block, and I was always excited to go to their house because their mom let them have Lucky Charms. They were a year older than me, though, and when they began kindergarten I saw them less and less. Until my brother was born I spent most of my time alone with my mom. We went to the park and made crafts. Even though there were not many kids around who were my age, my mother made sure I never felt lonely. She said that she loved playing with us when we were little because she got to watch us learn and grow.

My mom made our little second-floor apartment as cheerful as she could. She sewed yellow gingham curtains for the kitchen window and put an African violet on the windowsill. Later, she'd tell me that it was a lonely time for her, and with no direction of her own, the only thing she could think of to do was to have more children.

My dad got a job in Pittsburgh, and we moved across the state to Wexford. The gentle slopes and expansive farmland of eastern and central Pennsylvania gave way to the western Pennsylvania landscape of winding roads, steep inclines, and deep forests.

The phrase I heard about Wexford again and again from my parents and from the new parents and teachers they met when they enrolled us at St. Alexis Elementary School was that Wexford was a great place to raise kids; it was a great place to raise a family.

It was at this time in my life that, unbeknownst to me, my difference became an issue. Perhaps people see a five-year-old differently than they see a three- or four-year-old. Perhaps the fact that my family was enrolling me in school and moving to Wexford to stay made people nervous. The racism of otherwise benign and cordial white people began to rear its ugly head. Many years later, my dad revealed to me that shortly after we moved into our townhouse in Wexford, a woman called the house. My mother answered, and the woman hissed into the phone:

Nigger lover.

My mom had a black doctor at the time, and my parents reasoned that was what the heinous woman's call was about.

"We didn't even consider that it had anything to do with you," my dad said. It never crossed their minds that Wexford, this great place to raise children, might be unwelcoming for a child like me.

But maybe my parents did know that deep down. Maybe that's why in my teenage years my mother tried to steer me away from anything she thought was too black. It was around the time I entered kindergarten that people began asking me who I was and who my parents were, as if I needed to be vetted and accounted for.

When I was little, I never wore my hair down; my mother insisted that she fix it before going anywhere public. Usually, she parted it down the middle with the knife edge of a comb and slicked it into tight pigtails. I protested loudly as the stiff-bristled brush tore down my scalp. It was an act of love, but it also felt like vengeance.

She finally gave in to my eight-year-old demands to get a haircut. When the local hairdresser was finished, she swiveled me back toward the mirror. I saw my hair in a curly halo around my face, almost a perfect circle.

"I look like Mama from *Mama's Family*!" I said. I was too young to care about the style. I was just excited to have something new. My mom laughed. Contented, I got a lollipop, and we left the salon.

When I got home, my four-year-old brother, Patrick, was equally enthralled with my new style.

"You look like Eddie Murphy!" he said and started doing a dance. This time, my mom didn't laugh.

"No, she doesn't," my mother said, reprimanding my brother for an infraction he didn't understand. He stopped dancing.

From that time on and all throughout high school, my mother never let me get my hair cut again. I never understood why my brother's comment about my looking like Eddie Murphy made her angry—he seemed just as funny to me as *Mama's Family*.

Under the white gaze, race clings to people of color like a magnet to iron.

My parents pushed away the moments when race entered our lives because as far as they were concerned, race had nothing to do with them. It was not their business or concern. It was an unpleasant, impolite subject for other people to deal with. They avoided the discussion of race the same way they avoided the discussion of sex: it wasn't a proper subject for children. They deflected questions about race like they deflected questions about where babies come from. Like sex, race was the private business of other people; like sex, the subject of race had a sordid, forbidden tinge. My parents never talked to my brothers and me about the fact that there's a thing called race that divides people into different groups based on their skin color and heritage, yet somehow I knew these differences existed. They never talked to us about the cruelties of history based on the idea that because of their non-European origins, entire groups of people were considered less than human.

When race isn't explained to kids as an idea created by one group of people to subjugate another group, the distinctions between "black" and "white" seem inherent and natural. Growing up, the meaning of race was implied: normal people were white, dark-skinned people with African features were black, people with "slanted eyes" were Asian, and they were all fundamentally different from one another. My parents never told us explicitly that we were white, though that understanding was inherent in everything we did, how we looked at the world, and how the world looked at us. Except that wasn't true for me. When the world looked at me, no matter how much a part of my family I felt, no matter how comfortable I felt in my world, the magnet of the white gaze would pull me into conflict with someone else's ideas about whether or not I belonged.

In the summers, often with my young aunt and uncle, we vacationed on Long Beach Island, New Jersey, where my dad's father grew up. The house had blue siding with a long front porch and a yard filled with smooth white pebbles. When I was very young, my great-grandmother and great-aunt lived in a back room that was separated from the rest of the house. When we arrived, I was made to say hello to Nana (my great-grandmother) and Great-Aunt Betty, both of whom were small, emaciated, wheelchair-bound, and smelled of urine. Nana had dementia and smoked cigarettes with her gnarled hands, her eyes looking vacantly past me. Aunt Betty had had a stroke and only mumbled, "Bob is dead. Ruth is dead. Betty's dead." They terrified me.

I soon forgot the specters at the back of the house, though, as we packed up our gear, donned our flip-flops, and walked two blocks to the white sandy beach beyond the dunes. We'd make fun of the people who wore shoes and socks on the beach, calling them "shoobies." When we heard the ice cream truck jingle in the street, my brother and I would beg some change from our parents and run up the beach, hot sand giving way under our feet, to get our popsicles or ice cream sandwiches.

I loved those summers of making sandcastles and burying our feet in wet sand; collecting shells and hermit crabs at the water's edge; wading into the salty green ocean and braving the small swells. We'd stay out until our skin got dark and sweaty, pack up our gear, and go home for lunch.

My aunt was only five years older than I; when I was eight, she was thirteen. To me, she was the epitome of cool: a blond teenage beach babe in an OP bikini. Every time she went to the beach, usually with a surfer boyfriend, I begged to tag along.

One day, we were heading out with a tanned surfer boy who came to pick up my aunt. Before we left the house, she called back to me, "Bean, will you grab an extra towel?"

Bean, or Beaner, was a nickname my dad made up for me when I was a baby, as dads do. All my family members, including my aunt and uncle, called me Bean. As far as I knew, it came from the phrase "as cute as a bean." But it was the first my aunt's friend had heard it. To our surprise, he asked, "Do you call her *Bean* because she's dark like a coffee bean?"

I don't remember how my aunt responded. It seemed bizarre to me that my family nickname would refer to my skin color. After all, my whole family got tan in the summer. What made my tan so different? Only as an adult living in LA did I learn that the term *beaner* is a slur for Mexican immigrants. Though everyone in my family thought I was cute as a bean, for an outsider, the nickname took on a racial connotation.

No family is perfect. After we moved from Hickory Hills to Lincoln Boulevard, homelife became difficult. It was a chaotic time. My brother Thomas was born on May 17, 1986. Things became difficult for my mother. She described having two children as being manageable, but three was too many. Knight tore up the house and broke windows to bark at the paperboy. My dad was traveling more and more, leaving my stay-at-home mom with an increasingly unmanageable household.

During this time, my mother's anger often got the best of her and kept us in fear of making her lose her temper. Dragging me by the hair, the arm, or the leg and throwing things like a television or my brothers' clothes down the stairs were common occurrences. Not cleaning our rooms or leaving a backpack on the floor was always the straw that broke the camel's back. When my dad came home from work in the evening, he sat on the couch watching TV as though he were miles away. He didn't drink, he didn't yell, but after what was undoubtedly a long, stressful day at work, he was mentally and emotionally unavailable. Since my mother had had a long, stressful day at home but still had dinner to make, dishes to clean, clothes to fold, and kids to put to bed, every night they fought. The sound of my parents screaming at each other, my mother crying and yelling, "You'll all be sorry if I leave!" and, to my dad, "You're just going to run off with someone younger and thinner like your father did," was a nightly ritual.

She wasn't always angry, but I never knew which mother I was going to get: the happy, smiling mom, who fawned over me, told me how much she loved me, and got teary-eyed reminiscing about all the fun things we used to do as little kids, or the irate mother, who would threaten us at home and hiss through her teeth at me when we were in public, "Comb your hair," as if frizzy hair like mine could be combed.

When I was young, I always tried to play the peacemaker with my parents, but it rarely worked. I developed a diplomatic personality that was less focused on my own views and needs and more on the needs and views of those around me. I felt like an emotional translator, always trying to de-escalate the situations that made me uncomfortable. Because I wanted my parents' approval, especially my mother's, more than anything else, I tried my hardest to excel in every possible way—in school, in sports, and in appearance—to minimize conflict that I thought had something to do with me.

Twenty-four

Back at Princeton, I finally broke the news to my friends, telling them about what I'd been going through with my parents and the fact that I learned I had a black biological father. My friends weren't blind; they knew or suspected all along.

On the one hand, they were happy for me because they could see how relieved I was to finally learn the truth. On the other hand, they could see how emotional I was and how hurt and bewildered the whole situation made me feel. I had come out as black, and they supported me. David said when he came out to his family, their reaction was similar: they had known or suspected all along. His mother and his sisters were supportive, but his father was not. In my family, my father and my brothers were supportive, but my mother was not. I was glad I had such good friends—all white—who, even if they had never encountered the situation of someone switching races before, were committed to helping me through the transition.

To celebrate, they threw me a "coming out as black" party. Sveta and Angie came over with a gift bag. The card read, *Congratulations, you're black!*

When I opened the bag, I found a box of Dark & Lovely hair relaxer, a copy of *Black Hair* magazine, and a packet of Kool-Aid. They christened all of us with "black" names: Sveta became Chardonnay, her husband, Martin, became D'Martin, Angie became Aisha, and I became Sariqua. They were trying to share the experience with me and let me know that I was not alone in the only way they knew how, but at the same time, I realized that once again, my friends and I were making a joke out of the very blackness I wanted so desperately to embrace. We didn't know how else to deal with it. I didn't know what kind of response would have been more helpful at the time because I had little experience with what I considered authentic blackness myself. If I didn't know how to handle my transition or what to do, how could I expect that of my friends?

In private, though, my friends reached out to me with a gentler kind of humor.

In my gift bag, Angie included a "Happy Coming-Out-as-Black Day" card, as she put it. She wrote that she was impressed with the way I was handling everything and that I should celebrate my new-found heritage even though the circumstances were traumatic. She was glad I hadn't lost my sense of humor and thought I should embrace the rare opportunity of changing races. If I needed help, she wrote, she would always be there for me.

Her words meant a lot to me. Humor was always my coping mechanism. Being able to joke about a serious and traumatic situation made it easier for me to communicate about it and opened the way to more heartfelt expression. The gift bag items and the "black names" were stereotypical and went too far in turning blackness into a punch line, but I needed my friends now more than ever, and even if I was slightly offended by the gifts, it took a back seat to my need to be accepted.

I couldn't believe Angie thought I was handling things well. My life was changing so fast I couldn't pinpoint exactly what I was going through. Uncertainty and nervousness settled deep in my stomach and made my bowels tremble. The constant quivering took away my appetite, and anything I did eat I couldn't digest. I crawled into bed and stayed there as long as I could no matter the time of day, only getting up twice a week to go teach my Russian language class, which felt like torture. Even when I got home and crawled back to the safety of my bed, I couldn't relax. My head throbbed, and I was always cold.

At least my friends brought me out of my own private hell long enough to let me know they would help me in whatever way they could. Angie's letter offset the tone deafness of the gift basket and helped put what I was going through into perspective.

Abby, my friend from high school who had gone to Middlebury and was now living in Boston, wrote me a letter in her small, neat hand that included these lines:

> *This one is pretty tough. Just know that whatever a white girl from suburban PA can do for you, I totally will. (Wow, I feel like that was an insensitive remark or something. Just know that I didn't intend for it to be so. It's hard transitioning from "joke-mode" to "serious-mode" when it comes to you.)*

I didn't find her remark offensive at all. In fact, it was the first time one of my friends called out her own whiteness, and I appreciated it. In contrast to focusing on the blackness I now identified with, she focused on the whiteness from which I was becoming estranged.

Her letter also made me realize how difficult my armor of humor was to penetrate. We took Mr. Lynch's World Cultures class together. She was there when I was wrapped in an African cloth in front of everyone. Instead of talking about how we felt afterward, we joked about Buba. We joked about her Jewish father and Catholic mother, how she got double the holidays. Even now, my friends helped me through difficult times by throwing me a racist mock party.

My racial background was so fraught for me that I didn't know how to talk about it openly. When I talked to my parents about it, we fought. When I talked to my therapist, we seemed to be on different pages. At least my friends knew this was a big moment, the kind that divides your life into "before" and "after." The language of coming out was borrowed, but it symbolized that even if I always knew who I was deep down, and even if others could see the identity I was trying to hide, I no longer had to live a double life, denying who I was on the outside to keep others—in this case, my family—happy.

What my family didn't realize was that, as far of the rest of the world was concerned, I was already out. Even when people asked me about my background growing up, it was because they knew or suspected that I was not white. Most assumed I was at least partly African American.

When I was in high school, black boys were especially fond of me. When I went outside our small white community to the mall, to the amusement park, or to a basketball game with a rival school, I was often approached by young men who saw me as a light-skinned black girl. I was flattered by the attention they gave me because I didn't get that kind of interest from the boys at my school. If they seemed nice, I would give them my phone number. Eventually, a guy would call the house asking for me, and I'd have to explain to my mom who he was.

"You can't do that here!" she'd say about the possibility of me, her white teenage daughter, dating a black guy. "Not in this kind of neighborhood."

"What's wrong with it?" I'd ask. She never gave me a precise answer, only insisted that it—by which she meant interracial dating—wasn't acceptable. Though I didn't yet understand that I was mixed myself, the notion that interracial dating or marriage was not appropriate in our wholesome suburban community left me bewildered and angry. It didn't make sense to me that something as simple as two people from different ethnic backgrounds being together was looked down on as immoral or wrong.

All my years growing up, I was taught to believe something about myself other than what I saw in the mirror; that even though people assumed I was African American, they were wrong; that my community would not accept my dating a black boy because I was white. When it came to my own identity, I was so thoroughly taught to deny my own instincts that by the time I was in high school, I doubted my own sense of reality and relied on my family's story of who I was.

Thinking back on these experiences as I tried to integrate my multiple identities as an adult, I was angered by the gaslighting inherent in my parents' insistence on my whiteness. Recognizing the denial and conditioning to which I had been subject for so many years was the most difficult thing for me to come to terms with. How could they have lied to me for so long?

My parents acted as if they truly believed I was white, and when the news came that I had a different biological father, they both seemed genuinely surprised and dismayed. Did they lie to themselves as well so they could raise our family the way they wanted, the way they thought was best for us?

During those fights with my mom about whom I could and could not date, she seemed to wholeheartedly believe what she was saying. Her opposition to my involvement in interracial dating seemed earnest, which could have only been the case if in her racist mind she really believed I was white. Or did she just want that to be true, so much so that she created a truth in her own mind and inflicted it on the rest of us?

Did my dad just go along with it for his own sake, or was it a kind of folie à deux, a delusion shared by two? When the truth came out, my mother and father both assured me that they had never discussed my race. Even if that were true, I couldn't understand how it could go unremarked upon for so many years.

It remained difficult for me to grasp that at the same time my parents were teaching me to believe a lie about who I was, they were loving, supportive, and encouraging in every other way.

In second grade, they enrolled me in the school band program at my insistence and bought me the instrument I wanted to play: an alto saxophone. They listened to hours and hours of loud, terrible honking as I learned to play and attended all my grade-school concerts. It was just one example of how devoted they were to me as parents, and this made the idea that all along they had been subjecting me to psychological and emotional abuse even more difficult to accept.

How could both things be true? Did they even know they were doing it? Was my racial identity too wrapped up with a trauma my mother had willed herself to forget, thereby rewriting the whole family's history? Was my mislabeling just a symptom of a bigger system of denial in my family? Is it possible to gaslight someone unintentionally? How deep is the mind-set of racism?

As I asked myself these questions, I realized my mind was spinning, unable to even tell if the situation I was in with my family was emotionally abusive or not. I didn't trust my own evaluation of reality. Even more than the matter of what racial category I fell into, I couldn't get past the knowledge that my upbringing centered on a lie my parents consciously upheld regardless of the effect it might have on me. They were too busy being good parents to realize how deeply their racism and denial affected me.

My mother became extremely angry whenever the topic of race came up, while my dad calmly explained that race was simply not our problem. In both cases, I felt bullied, confused, and full of doubt. When I did try to assert how I felt, it was dismissed as teenage rebellion. Because I trusted my parents implicitly, because of how close we were as a family, because of all that they had done for me over the years, I couldn't even conceive of the fact that they would lie to me, that they had known the truth all along.

Despite our arguments, growing up, I trusted my mother's judgment. I'm not the kind of person who makes a lot of casual acquaintances, because I don't trust many people. I'm socially introverted and have a close circle of friends I have known for a long time. I am confident speaking in front of a crowd of people but shy away from unstructured contact with those same people. I tend to have long-term relationships but will end or sabotage a relationship before someone has a chance to betray my trust. When I found out that my mother, the person I trusted most in the world, had been lying to me for years, emotionally and psychologically, it was too much for me to handle.

After my friends went home and the coming-out party ended, I sat huddled in bed paging through *Black Hair* magazine. I marveled at the creative, sometimes gravity-defying hairstyles, complex braids, and heads bursting with spiral curls. I realized, somewhat sadly, that most of the hairstyles pictured would not really work on me. My hair's texture could not hold a true Afro and was too limp to wear straightened or in cornrows.

I went to the salon in high school to have my hair fixed in a French braid for homecoming. Because of my hair's texture and fineness, the braid tapered to a skinny rattail at the end. When I got home, I took the braid out and wore my hair the way I usually did—with the front pulled back and the rest hanging suspended above my shoulders. The moment that was supposed to be fun and exciting for a teenage girl—getting her hair done at a salon for a high school dance—just reminded me that the long, full, highlighted braids that graced the tanned necks of the other girls at the dance were beyond me.

I didn't really know how to take care of my hair; it was an uneven mass when I let it down, and I usually wore it brushed into a tight ponytail. It grew to around my shoulders and then would break off, frizzing out on top and at the ends. I realized I would never have hair like the women modeling the hairstyles in *Black Hair*. Nevertheless, I wanted to do something different with my hair to signal the change that was happening on the inside.

I researched curly hair patterns online and discovered that my hair was somewhere between type 3B and 3C. 3B hair had springy ringlets that dried fluffy without any products to add moisture and definition. 3C hair had tight corkscrew curls and tended to fluff up even more, like an Afro. Its curl made it brittle, and it broke easily at the ends. The description of 3C hair reminded me of the issues I had with my own hair: breaking off when it grew shoulder length, looking puffy and undefined if I wore it down. I was excited to see that the photo of the girl with 3C hair looked like me. She was black but mixed. Some of the girls with 3B hair were white. Others were non-white, maybe Latina or another ethnicity. Both hair types needed daily conditioning, deep conditioning weekly, and curl-defining products to look their best. I learned about the natural hair movement, how women of color were taking a stand against a society that wanted them to conform by wearing straightened hair and long straight weaves. These women proudly wore their hair the way it grew out of their heads, whether kinky, coiled, zigzagged, or corkscrewed. They embraced shorter, naturally styled hair, which was easier to keep healthy, instead of opting to damage their hair through heat styling, straightening, and relaxing.

I wanted to be part of the movement. Through learning about my hair I began to form an idea of mixed identity for the first time. My hair revealed my African American and Italian heritage. When my hair was wet, I could wind a small section around my finger and make a perfect corkscrew curl. When it dried, I could separate those curls, but instead of producing layers of thick satiny springs like the curly hair I saw in conditioner ads, the ends would fly away, and the top and bottom layers hung at different angles. I wasn't sure of what ethnicity my complexion and features showed, but I was familiar with my hair. It had been with me my whole life, and it was always the same. Most of the time, I related to my hair with frustration, but now I saw redefining my relationship with my hair as an opportunity to settle into my new sense of identity.

As important as my hair journey was at this point, I realized my hair was not the only way I would be able to prove or affirm my blackness. Even though I was conflicted about what he meant to me, the only way I thought I could connect directly to my own blackness was to find my biological father. Only by standing beside an African American who was biologically related to me would I be able to show the world and myself that I was unequivocally black. Maybe then, my family would acknowledge it, too.

This father I didn't know, who used to be just an idea, a hint, a shadow, was becoming much more. He was becoming the only real way for me to truly know myself. Because I believed he'd raped my mother, I had mixed feelings about wanting to have a relationship if and when I found him, but I was still overwhelmed by curiosity. Would we like the same things? Would he look like me? Would I become part of a whole family I never knew I had? These questions and more kept me up at night, wondering. More than anything, though, I wanted to see him not as a menacing threat but as a real live human being. I regretted that, because of my mother's experience, I never had the chance to decide for myself how he would be part of my life. My mother saw any hint of my wanting to know who he was as a deep betrayal. "How could you even think that after what he did to me?" she said. I knew it was wrong, but I couldn't help it. How much of her trauma was I supposed to take on as my own? I became obsessed with his reality, his blackness as my blackness. I thought that without him, I would always remain incomplete.

Over the next few years, to discover what it meant to be black in America, I looked for the answer in books I could relate to, like *The Book of American Negro Poetry* and *Creating Black Americans*, a textbook by Nell Painter that traces the history of African American art. I read memoirs about wrestling with mixed identity and family secrets: Bliss Broyard's *One Drop*, Danzy Senna's *Where Did You Sleep Last Night?*, and James McBride's *The Color of Water*. I had a lot of time and ignorance to make up for. I could hear my mother's standard summation of race and racism—*It just affects so few people*—but these were real experiences of real people. No matter what their percentage of our country's overall population, their experience and mine mattered.

But I couldn't learn what it means to be black from a textbook.

I always knew I could pass for black, but that's all I thought it was.

Now, years later, I began to realize that light-skinned and mixed-race black folks had passed for white throughout our country's history, often as a means of survival and to take advantage of privileges like interracial marriage, jobs, and education that were denied to those classified as black. I learned about the one-drop rule instituted during Jim Crow that required anyone with even one black ancestor to identify as black, so as to keep the white race pure. I learned about the brown paper bag test, a measure for determining whether or not an individual was allowed certain privileges based on whether or not their skin color was lighter or darker than a brown paper bag. I learned how that engendered colorism among African Americans, leading lighter-skinned men, and especially women, to be considered more beautiful, desirable, and upwardly mobile. I began to realize that because my complexion was light enough and my features European enough, it was easier for my parents to let me pass for white than to be honest about my background, and when anyone asked about it, they simply didn't answer. It occurred to me that maybe ever since I was an infant, their desire to start a family of their own, despite the odds, was so strong that when they looked at me, they looked past the parts of me that didn't match up with their ideal. They didn't look at me and see me. They looked at me and saw themselves.

Once I made it clear that I identified as black, old friends came out of the woodwork to write to me on Facebook and talk about the fact that they'd always known, or suspected, that I was adopted. They had known I didn't look like the rest of my family members. I had been conditioned to think I didn't look "black enough," and that's why I could have gone for so long believing I was white. I had been mistaken for so many different ethnicities over the course of my lifetime that it was difficult for me to accept that I looked identifiably black, even though that certainty was something I'd always longed for. Now I had to develop a sense of black and mixed identity that accounted for both my European features and my African ones.

I became hyperaware of how others perceived me, and it became more difficult for me to shrug off comments directed at my racial difference, comments which, growing up, I'd simply tuned out. I recalled the time in high school when the other school's track team taunted me; it hadn't registered to me then that they were all white and the words they were yelling were racial slurs. But the knowledge and the anger that came with it that was stuck somewhere deep in my subconscious now lodged free. Now, when a white grad student asked me why someone like me would be interested in studying Slavic literature, or when the lecturer for whom I was a teaching assistant told me he was glad to be teaching with someone "less male and less white" than he was, I felt the same way I did back then, an anger I didn't know how to counter or express. But I was now at least aware of that anger.

Twenty-five

In the months after I learned about my biological father, I had to do something more decisive than change my hair to break with the version of myself that had been hurt, disappointed, and betrayed by my family.

I decided to change my name.

I wanted my new name to reflect my African American identity, something that belonged to me and wasn't determined by my family. I thought about changing my first and last names, but I immediately discarded that idea. Changing both my names made it seem like I was a fugitive, someone who wanted to bury the past and build a new identity from the ground up. There was something furtive about it. I didn't want to become another person; I had already become one. I didn't need to erase my entire identity to know that.

I always liked the name *Kenya*, which I came across in college as the first name of one of the Spanish professors, Kenya Dworkin. She was white (or looked white), but to me, her name was evocative of African heritage. The problem was that I didn't know where in Africa my ancestors were from. After I took the paternity test with my dad,

I ordered another DNA test on my own that would show me the breakdown of my ancestry. The results showed I was 45 percent European, 45 percent sub-Saharan African, and 10 percent Asian. Unfortunately, the pie chart graph of my genetics was not more detailed and only showed origins by continental region, not by ethnic group or even country.

Could I change my first name? Could I get used to going by a different name from the one I'd had my whole life? I wasn't particularly fond of the name *Sarah* when I was younger; I thought it was too common. There were always one or two other Sarahs in my class. Some spelled it without the *h*, and they always struck me as imposters. As I grew, I came to identify with the name. After all, my father would remind me, *Sarah* meant *princess*. The biblical Sarah, Abraham's wife, was originally named *Sarai*, which meant *quarrelsome*. I thought both meanings fit me well.

When I thought about it, Kenya seemed a bit on the nose. Even though I loved the sound of that name, I knew I would feel like I was trying too hard to impose an African identity on myself. It felt like other people would realize that, too. Should I change my middle name to Kenya? My middle name was Elizabeth, the name of my father's mother. It felt too stuffy, and lately when I was asked on forms to fill out my whole name, I would drop the *Elizabeth* and just write *Sarah Dunn*. Changing my middle name would be too safe, I decided, since it was a name you could choose to use or not. I wasn't going to require people to address me as Sarah Kenya—which sounded pretty terrible anyway—so the only one who would know I had a different middle name from the one I was given would be me.

That left only one option: to change my last name. It was the name that tied me most to my family; my father's family name, the name my mother took when she married, the name I shared with my

brothers. If my parents insisted that the revelation didn't change anything for our family, then changing my last name should not, either.
It was a way of signaling my independence to help me move on emotionally and psychologically. It was a way of differentiating myself
from the little girl who believed what her parents told her and wanted
nothing more than to be a good daughter. That girl was still a part of
me, but it didn't embody who I was today. I could hold the "before"
and "after" parts of myself in one whole by giving myself a new last
name.

I couldn't change my last name to reflect my biological father
because I didn't know who he was. I wasn't sure I would take his name
even if I did; changing my name wasn't about adopting a new family.
I wanted to become fully integrated with myself, with all the complexities and inconsistencies that would entail.

I visited the Tretyakov Gallery during my first semester abroad in
Moscow. I lived in an apartment in the southern reaches of the city
just inside the third ring, a few blocks from Danilov Monastery. My
metro stop was Tulskaya on the gray line. I trekked to the metro and
took the escalator down into the large, empty station. Tulskaya didn't
connect to any other stops, and most of the time there were few, if
any, other people on the platform. I knew I looked strange to my
neighbors, who were mostly old Russians, but after living in the massive city for five months, I learned to ignore the stares, or stare back.
I carved out my own routes and routines, getting around via the
metro, the trolley when I was downtown, the *elektrichka* when I
wanted to go to the far outskirts, and on foot. That day, the platform
was empty except for an old woman sweeping the already gleam-
ing marble floor with a handmade broom. These women, bent and

kerchiefed, were eternal denizens of the subway stations, keeping them spotless with only a coarse straw broom and sometimes a rag on the end of a stick despite the millions of feet that traversed them each day.

Tulskaya was not one of the vaulted high-ceilinged stations downtown that was tiled floor and ceiling in intricate patterns with massive statues of Soviet heroes placed at the entrances. The work of Stalin, they looked like underground cathedrals to Soviet power, and they were awe-inspiring. Tulskaya was built in the 1980s and had a simpler design. Marble walls transitioned to art deco designs that extended up the slightly arched white ceiling. Dropped light fixtures shaped like diamonds ran the length of the station, with wooden benches separating the northbound and southbound sides of the platform.

It was May, and the mounds of exhaust-covered snow that flanked the roads were melting into deep gray pools. The sky was sunny but icy cold. Being a foreigner, I quickly shed my winter layers as soon as the sun came out. Muscovites around me gave me sidelong stares as they trundled by wrapped in thick winter coats. They knew the weather could turn at any point. It was a bad idea to trust the sun.

To get to the museum, I took the gray line and transferred to Dobryninskaya station on the ring. The city of Moscow is built as a sequence of concentric rings, that lead to the heart of the city at Red Square. The ring line on the metro transfers to every other line and can get you any place downtown. The metro stations along this line were the first to be built and are the most ornate.

Dobryninskaya was one of the original stations built in 1950, with marble arches, a dark marble floor, and a high ceiling. The architects took inspiration from the interiors of ancient Russian Orthodox churches but balanced those features with twelve bas-reliefs of Soviet workers from different nationalities and three floor-to-ceiling mosaics over a hundred feet tall of Lenin and parading soldiers of the Red Army.

From Dobryninskaya, I transferred to Oktyabrskaya, where the ring line and the orange line connect. Oktyabrskaya was named for the October Revolution of 1917. At first, I thought the bas-relief figures on the ceiling in flowing cloaks holding laurels and trumpets aloft were angels. The laurel wreaths carved into the ceiling were topped with the Soviet star, hammer, and sickle. One of the figures carved on the colossal station's marble façade wore a helmet and flowing cape, raising his Kalashnikov to heaven.

I knew I was getting close to the museum because the station where I disembarked, Tretyakovskaya, named for the gallery above, was decorated with plaques depicting great Russian painters.

The sprawling red-and-white brick building that housed the gallery looked like a gingerbread castle out of a Russian fairy tale. In a cupola crowning the façade was a rendering of the famous sixteenth-century icon, St. George Killing the Dragon.

In my program for foreign students at the Russian State University for the Humanities, we were studying Russian painters. Our assignment was to write a report on a painting from the Tretyakov Gallery. I knew the painter I wanted to study, but I hadn't yet picked out a painting.

In the modernist hall, past works by Kandinsky, Malevich, and Natalia Goncharova, was a painting of a bull swimming away in the ocean. In a white wake, the long-horned bull swam confidently among the waves, filling the center of the painting. On its back, a dark-haired woman balanced as if deciding whether or not to take her chances with the bull or throw herself into the sea. The image struck me as odd. The colors were bright, done in a broad-stroked style that seemed naïve. The bull was brown with white spots and long horns, the ocean and sky nearly the same shade of blue. The swells and ripples were rendered in thick blue strokes to show motion; two dolphins arched through waves in the background. It looked like a child drew them.

The scene was complicated, though. The woman on the bull's back wore a black dress, and her face was inscrutable. She looked unsteady; her knees sloped dangerously close to the churning water, her feet flexed as if readying her to jump. The bull is swimming away, but its head is turned back to look at the woman. I didn't know why, but the image felt menacing. The waves seemed to rise toward the viewer, rather than into the distance. The perspective made the viewer feel like the sea was all around them. It took me a moment to realize that while the bull was looking back at the woman, he was looking at me, too. He gazes knowingly at us, making the viewer complicit in the woman's fate.

The painting was *The Rape of Europa* by the Russian painter Valentin Serov and depicts the Greek myth of Zeus, transformed into a bull, who captures a beautiful Phoenician woman named Europa and carries her across the sea to the island of Crete, where he rapes and impregnates her. I knew the classical version of the story painted by Titian in 1560. In that painting, Europa writhes violently on the bull's back, her clothes in disarray. The meaning of the painting is unambiguous; she is being taken against her will. Cherubs reach for her from the sky, but their efforts are in vain. Although she is still near the shore, she cannot escape.

Serov painted his version in 1910, and the scene is both ambiguous and hopeless. Instead of cherubs in the sky, there are two dolphins who are blind to the situation, their heads in the water. The shore is nowhere in sight, the entire canvas taken up by the rising waves. Zeus is not the enticing white bull in the myth but a more realistic shade of dark brown. Europa's clothes are black instead of white, and she is not writhing or screaming like in Titian's version. She knows she is lost and is deciding what to do: take her chances with the bull or throw herself into the waves. There is no one to save her. Instead of displaying classical drama, Serov's painting evokes quiet menace. The bull's look is one of cold aggression. He knows that we know. And like the dolphins and Europa, there is nothing we can do to stop it.

I stood in front of the painting in the Tretyakov Gallery in awe of the feelings of serenity, resignation, beauty, and terror it kindled. A well-known figurative painter, Valentin Serov always left a clue, a wink to the viewer in his paintings. A knowing eye catches you in its cross-hairs, like the horse in his 1897 painting of Grand Duke Pavel Alexandrovich Romanov. A decorated aristocrat stands in the foreground in his Imperial military uniform. He wears a golden cuirass emblazoned with red; heavy gold epaulettes with long tassels adorn his shoulders; and a gold sculpture of an eagle, the symbol of Imperial Russia, is attached to each of his gauntlets. Though the image is supposed to be regal, the slim figure of the grand duke seems overwhelmed by his uniform's awkward grandeur. His eyes stare vacantly into the distance. A dark brown horse stands close behind him, its head turned so that one eye looks directly at the viewer. The look is one of irony, as if even the horse knows the aristocrat is not as glorious or courageous as his royalty and rank would have us believe. In *The Rape of Europa*, the joke turns sinister when you realize that by meeting the bull's gaze, you've given consent for what is about to happen.

My trip to the Tretyakov Gallery and my fascination with Valentin Serov stayed with me over the years. As I thought about changing my name in a way that truly embodied my own experience, not determined by my family or the ethnicity they chose for me, I recalled the painting.

I was more than my biological heritage on both sides of my family. Even though the last name *Valentine* sounded Anglo, I knew where my inspiration came from. My experiences in Moscow—riding the metro, making the city my own—created a world of memories and knowledge that no one could take away.

Even though the name change was liberating for me, there was an unintended consequence—it hurt my father's feelings.

One day when I was home for vacation, my dad picked me up from the airport. We drove in silence for a while, and then he said, "Family is about loyalty."

"I know," I said, "but . . . ," and I launched into my explanation about why changing my name was important to me. He didn't say anything after that. In fact, he never mentioned my changed last name again, but I knew what he meant, and I knew I had crossed a line.

At first, my mother supported me changing my name. I was surprised, because she seemed wary of my desire to evolve my sense of identity.

"A woman should have her own name," she said, perhaps reflecting on her own choice. In the past, she'd told me that she hated when people wrote her letters or addressed her as *Mrs.* Later, she switched to *Ms.* in her correspondence, leaving her marital status undisclosed.

The feeling of sisterhood did not last long, maybe because she realized my father felt betrayed. She told me it was selfish, that I was choosing someone I didn't know over our family, over my father who was the best father I could ever wish for. I tried to explain that I wasn't choosing someone else, I was choosing me, but she could only see it as me creating more distance between my family and myself.

Twenty-six

Walking into the library one day during my final year of grad school, I saw a poster advertising a poetry reading. I stopped and stared at the photo of the poet—a handsome mixed-race man with salt-and-pepper hair, kind, intelligent eyes, and a warm smile. I had never heard of him, but I knew that I'd be attending the reading that evening.

His name was Michael. I became even more enchanted when I attended the event and heard him read. In a lilting British accent, Michael read poems that were romantic yet unflinching from life's uncomfortable complexities. After the reading, he signed a book for me, even though I was a broke grad student and couldn't afford it. Being shy, I ran away before we could have a conversation.

The next day, I looked up his home university and emailed to thank him. I gave him my number. We emailed back and forth, talked on the phone, and, since he lived in Los Angeles, we met up when he had readings on the East Coast, in D.C. or New York. On our first date, at a little Japanese restaurant in lower Manhattan, he told me about his experience being half-English and half-Nigerian, about growing up during the Biafran War, fleeing a repressive government in his home country, moving to London and feeling like an outsider, and finally finding a home in the United States.

As I listened to his story, I felt like Michael was a person to whom I could tell anything, who would immediately understand my conflicts with family and identity even though they were somewhat different from his own. I told him about what happened to my mother. It was the first time I'd uttered the words *I am a child of rape*.

Part of me wasn't sure if that were true, but my mother's insistence on being violated made it the only explanation for my conception that I had.

The first night Michael and I spent together, I cried tears I never thought I'd be able to share with anyone.

In the spring he moved to Princeton, and we lived together while I finished my dissertation.

One day we were driving in New Brunswick and spotted an African shop.

"Let's stop here," he said. "I want to see something."

We parked and got out of the car.

It was a salon, which to me looked sketchy, with a few pieces of glossy black-and-red furniture left over from the '90s. Strands of long black hair littered the floor. In the corner near the front window was a filmy display case that featured long bags of synthetic hair, DVDs with covers that looked homemade, and a tangle of other items that blended together before my eyes. The store was empty except for a black girl about eight years old sitting on one of the chairs next to a side table covered with magazines.

A disinterested woman sat behind the counter. It was the kind of place I'd seen many times in passing but never considered entering. As Michael entered the shop with full confidence, I felt unsafe, like

I was some place I wasn't supposed to be. *What can he want in a salon like this?* I was nervous, though I tried to act nonchalant. He greeted the woman behind the counter in pidgin, so different from the educated, British-inflected language I was used to hearing from him. The woman was also from Nigeria and was Igbo like him. Because of his mixed background and lighter skin, she was skeptical of his identity.

He spoke Igbo to her, and she asked him in English, "You are African?"

He said yes.

Then, unexpectedly, she turned to me and asked, "Are *you* African?"

Distracted from my reverie, I said, "No!"

They both laughed out loud.

Apparently, I gave away my discomfort by my emphatic and surprised response. Michael got what he had come for—a few Nollywood DVDs—and we left. I was just getting used to the idea of being black and being mixed, but I couldn't conceive of my being African.

How could I connect with the roots of American blackness if I didn't know what it meant to be African? I was ashamed that I had quickly and automatically disavowed any relation to what I unconsciously perceived as an inferior identity. "Don't confuse me with that!" my response said. "I don't belong there!"

Michael was a culturally fluid, multilingual professor and writer. His identity included black, mixed race, Igbo, British, and American, though these distinctions sometimes merged or conflicted with one another. His family was ethnically Igbo, and their lineage could be traced back to the founding of Afikpo, the village in which he grew up. He did not have to contend with the erasures of the Middle

Passage: his identity was grounded in an ethnicity that had its own ancestral state.

He explained that the "village" of Afikpo had a population of over two hundred thousand, making it around the same size as the city of Pittsburgh, where I grew up, and which, to him, accounted for my unrefined "bush" ways. I'd always pictured an African village as a collection of thatched huts connected by a few dirt roads, with women cooking over open fires and washing clothes in a nearby river. In reality, it was a large, complex community. As an educated middle-class family with a white mother, his family enjoyed status and privilege that I imagined had been reserved for white colonials. Michael said that when he showed up to school in second grade, he was the only student who had a pen, and the teacher sent him home for being arrogant.

Despite having been paraded in front of my high school World Cultures class dressed in a Nigerian wrapper as an example of the "African woman," I knew nothing about the real lives of people from African cultures. I had a mountain of prejudice and shame to overcome before I could embrace those aspects of myself and how they squared with my decidedly white, middle-American upbringing.

How could two identities that existed so far apart reside in a single person? And what about African American identity? How did that relate to Africanness?

I defended my dissertation in the spring and felt like St. George slaying a dragon I'd wrestled with for six years. I was triumphant, elated, and exhausted. I not only survived the trials of graduate school, but passed with flying colors. I felt like a true expert on my subject as I sat at the head of the once-threatening huge mahogany seminar table surrounded by the most elite professors in my field.

During my defense, Michael was the only other dark-skinned face in the room, and I was grateful that my stuffy, self-important professors had to cope with the presence of this much more widely known and celebrated writer and that he was on my team, so to speak. For the first time in my six years of grad school, and for the first time in my life, I felt like the majority. There were only the two of us, but we could not be ignored.

Twenty-seven

Backstage at Richardson Auditorium amid the throng of black-clad bodies, I adjusted my graduation robes. My mother had paid the $800 needed to get me the high-quality doctoral regalia: a black robe made of heavy fabric with thick orange velvet chevrons on the sleeves, large orange stripes down the front, a blue velvet hood, and a black velvet four-sided hat with a gold tassel.

"You'll need them for graduation ceremonies when you're a professor," she said, "It was always my dream for you to go to Princeton."

I thanked her over the phone. Even though my graduate fellowship, teaching, writing center tutoring, and research assistantships, paid for most of my school, it was never quite enough, and my parents helped me financially all through grad school. In graduating with my doctorate, I felt like I had made good on their faith in me, but like all the support they gave me throughout my life, it was a debt I could never repay.

I straightened my hair with a new flatiron I'd bought from the Home Shopping Network, which showed women of various ethnicities having their hair turned from curly or frizzy into straight, sleek cascades. It was the first one I'd ever bought, and while I was getting ready, I was surprised by the sizzle and steam when the hot irons clamped down on my still-wet curls. As I pulled the burning irons down my hair and away from my scalp, I was amazed at the light, straight wisps that emerged; I thought the already ridiculous-looking puffy hat I'd have to wear would look much better over straight, sleek tresses than over my natural hair.

Graduate students, undergraduates, and their parents milled around in anticipation backstage, and they were all members of the African diaspora, including me. There was such a feeling of pride as the younger students and their parents looked at the black students receiving their doctoral degrees. Parents of undergrads looked at me and my doctoral hood and smiled or nodded proudly. For the first time, I felt seen as both a high-achieving scholar and a black woman. I was part of the black excellence filling the auditorium and not a token for the white gaze. The ceremony was a witnessing for us, our friends, and families.

The event was organized by the Black Graduate Caucus. I'd thought about joining the group when I first came out, but I didn't quite know how or if I would fit in. I still felt like an outsider in black social groups.

The organizer, a light-skinned woman with perfectly quaffed shoulder-length hair and a professional demeanor, came by to get my name and check me off the list of participants. We greeted each other and shook hands; we'd only met a couple of times before. Maybe she wondered why, after six years at Princeton, I had suddenly popped out of the woodwork, why I hadn't attended any Black Caucus meetings or events before. At the start of the year, I had gotten an email from the group about a Black and Brown Barbecue they were hosting to kick off the school year.

"Do you want to go?" I asked a friend who studied in the Slavic department. She was of Indian descent.

"Can I go?" she asked.

"Well, you're brown, aren't you?" I responded, assuming she was comfortable with that descriptor.

"Am I?" she asked. I wasn't sure how to respond. We left it at that, and I did not attend the event. I wondered why my friend, who to my eyes was brown-skinned and a minority, did not identify as such. We were the only two nonwhite students in the Slavic department at the time and traded stories about professors referring to us as "exotic" and making comments about our hair and eyes.

At the pan-African graduation ceremony, we would receive a black stole embroidered with the Princeton crest; red, yellow, and green stripes; and our graduation year, and we could wear this stole as part of our university-wide graduation ceremony the next day.

We filed into our seats as the lights in the auditorium dimmed. I sat next to Patrice, a Jamaican doctoral student with long locks and glasses, from the history department. I was excited, and I fidgeted with the program in my hands. In my six years at Princeton, it would be the first time I could stand up and be counted in this group. Was my experience at Princeton more difficult because of my ethnicity? Were my struggles personal or collective, or both? Did we share Africa's history of disenfranchisement, even if we never experienced that hardship ourselves? Students participating in the ceremony came from different countries, social classes, and educational backgrounds. Some were from wealthy, elite families while some were first-generation college students. Between my defense and graduation, I went home to visit my grandparents. My grandmother, who never went to college and spent her life as a homemaker, had a rare tear in her eye as she said, "When you get your diploma, a little part of me is up there with you."

Maybe graduating with other members of the African diaspora meant that our success didn't just affect the future but also the past and the lives of those who came before us. The ceremony's theme was "Sankofa: Looking Back to Move Forward." *Sankofa* is a Ghanaian term that translates as "Go back and get it" and is the source of the proverb "It is not wrong to go back for that which you have forgotten." You can't know where you're going unless you know where you've been. The symbol for Sankofa is a stork-like bird with its long neck reaching backward while its feet face forward. It carries a small egg in its mouth, a precious seed containing the past and future.

The presenters walked out onto the lit stage and stood beside a table on which lay our stoles. I had entered Princeton as a white student too scared to question my family's founding myth, and I was leaving as an African American, mixed-race woman with a hard-won sense of self, determined not to take the stories of the world for granted.

An African dance troupe twirled onstage to the sound of drums, swirling in costumes of blue, yellow, and red. The rhythm, music, and dance were contagious, but observing the formality of the occasion, we all sat firmly in our seats. When the dancers had finished, the presenter said, "Now we will rise and sing the Black National Anthem."

The what?

I rose with everyone else as they began to sing a beautiful but solemn a cappella hymn. I had never heard the song before. I looked around and saw that no one was looking at the programs, in which the lyrics were printed. Everyone in the auditorium seemed to know the song by heart. I grew warm under my heavy robe as I mouthed words I didn't know and tried to pick up the tune. Would the people sitting around me realize I didn't know this song? I didn't even know there was a Black National Anthem. I had not learned this song in school or church. It was never part of my courses on American history. It wasn't sung before baseball or football games; it did not play at the Olympics when our athletes won gold. I caught some of the words as I hummed along:

Sing a song full of the faith that the dark past has taught us.
Sing a song full of the hope that the present has brought us . . .

I couldn't catch it all. The lyrics were dark but hopeful. No dewy-eyed patriotism for the stars and stripes, no glorification of bloodshed or awe at the weapons of war; just the knowledge that our ancestors endured unspeakable horror and that we continue to hope and strive for true freedom.

How does one weigh the balance of genetics versus lived experience in the equation of cultural belonging? I studied the Russian language for years, studied its literature, culture, history, and people. I lived among Russians on my own and in Russian homes from Moscow to Kamchatka. I could distinguish regional dialects and mannerisms. I knew what Siberians thought of Muscovites and vice versa. I could write, watch soap operas, and dream in Russian. I could talk to dogs and cats like Russians did, even naming myself after my favorite Russian painter. And now I was getting a degree from one of the top schools in the world that ratified my expertise in the realm of Russian language and literature. My knowledge was almost as deep as a native's. But that didn't make me Russian.

Onstage, the speaker announced my name. The graduate next to me, Patrice, swung his legs around so I could get out of the row of seats. I walked onstage, smiled, shook the presenters' hands, and lowered my head so one of them could place the stole around my neck.

After the ceremony, I was full of questions and thoughts. I wanted to talk to Angie, who had sat in the audience during the ceremony to cheer me on, about the experience I'd just had. We met near the auditorium doors as everyone filed out and stepped into the early June sun. I was about to speak when she said, "So, if a white person from Africa wanted to participate in this ceremony, they wouldn't be allowed to?"

The question was so far from my mind I didn't know how to answer. It was strange that after such a strong display of black excellence, pan-African community, and culture, that was the thing on her mind. I changed the subject to where we would go to dinner the next night, and we decided on Ethiopian.

Twenty-eight

I spent my last days at Princeton wandering around the town with a sense of nostalgia and deep, gnawing confusion. The stately brick and Tudor houses—some more like mansions—the maple-lined streets, and manicured lawns were beautiful, I thought, and I envisioned a future for myself in which, armed with my prestigious degree, passion for teaching, and undeniable expertise in the field of post-Soviet neo-avant-garde Russophone poetics, I would one day inhabit such a fine dwelling and lead a peaceful, affluent, intellectual life.

Even as I fantasized about my professorial future, a nagging thought burst to the forefront of my mind: *Shouldn't I hate all this?* The smug superiority that oozed from every beveled window, the hypocrisy of a town that prided itself on its quaint charm but outsourced its upkeep to workers who couldn't afford to live there. The false humility of a university whose motto was "In the nation's service," but who hoarded its multibillion-dollar endowment like a dragon.

Like most elite universities in the country, Princeton did not admit blacks or women until the second half of the twentieth century.

In my search to discover how my identity fit into my life, I came across a 1910 report titled *The College-Bred Negro American* edited by W. E. B. Du Bois. The editor queried various elite institutions as to whether or not they admitted black students.

The replies were dismissive. Johns Hopkins responded, "No colored man has ever been a candidate for a degree here."

A representative from Bryn Mawr asserted, "[No] person of Negro descent has ever applied for admission to Bryn Mawr College, probably because the standard of entrance examinations is very high and no students are admitted on certificate."

Princeton's response was a study in ambivalence: "The question of the admission of Negro students has never assumed the aspect of a practical problem with us. We have never had any colored students here, though there is nothing in the University statutes to prevent their admission.

"It is possible, however, in view of our proximity to the South, and the large number of southern students here, that Negro students would find Princeton less comfortable than some other institutions."

I heard the same argument from Russians about why racism did not exist in their country; an absence of black folks equaled an absence of racism. In the universities and in Russia, no one thought about the circumstances that occasioned the lack of black people in the first place.

I learned through other sources that Princeton admitted its first four black male students as undergraduates in 1945 as part of a military-sponsored program. The university took over two more decades to admit women, beginning in 1969, not primarily to further gender equity or because it believed in the intellectual equality of men and women, but to keep pace with its rival Yale, which had become coeducational a year earlier.

I could not find any data on when the first black women came to Princeton—whether it was with that first graduating female class of 1973, or if others who were light-skinned had managed to pass under the radar before that, as Anita Hemmings had done at Vassar in 1897. When Hemmings's roommate found out through a private investigator that Hemmings was African American, the roommate was so traumatized that Hemmings was made to reside in a separate room until graduation. Hemmings was considered the class beauty, and rumors circulated that her dark hair and olive features came from Indian blood. Hemmings and her husband, who was also light enough to pass, never disclosed their racial heritage to their children.

I found a short description of one incoming freshman's experience at Princeton University in the 1930s, which suggested again that, though nothing in the laws of the college prevented their admission, African Americans were decidedly not welcome.

A student named Bruce Wright applied, was admitted, and even won a scholarship to Princeton's undergraduate program. Presumably, there was no box to check on the application for race or ethnicity, and the admissions office did not know they had granted a coveted spot in their program to a black student. When he showed up for registration and his race was discovered, he was promptly dismissed by the dean of admissions, Radcliffe Heermance, who claimed his entrance scores were not high enough to grant him a place in the freshman class.

Dean Heermance went on to write a letter explaining that no colored student ever attended Princeton, but there were many Southern students, which was a tradition at the school, and that Wright would be uncomfortable since "as you know there is still a feeling in the south quite different from that existing in New England." Though the dean admitted he had "very pleasant relations with your race, in civilian life and in the army," he could not advise Wright to attend Princeton, stating that he would be happier at a school with members of his own race. In the margin of that letter, Wright wrote: "Damn the pleasant relationship; I want to go to college." In a moment of insight and maybe even compassion, the dean wrote: "A member of your race might feel very much alone."

Wright became a judge, eventually serving on New York's Supreme Court. Princeton's class of 2001 made him an honorary member, and he was profiled in the documentary project *Blacks at Princeton: The Black Experience at Princeton from 1746 to the Present*.

I entered my graduate program at Princeton having checked the box under race or ethnicity marked "White." After coming out, my friends told me that our program administrator had asked them about my race when I arrived in the department. She wanted to double-check that I was the person listed on my admission form. My classmates covertly scrutinized me and concluded that since I didn't sound black or seem to identify as such, despite their suspicions, I must be white. Or white enough.

The difference between Anita Hemmings and me was that I lived in a different time. It was still true that African Americans at Princeton or schools like it "might feel very much alone," but we were not forbidden from attending. When I formally changed my name and racial identity with the university and my department, no scandal ensued. I was met with unsympathetic dismissiveness by most of my professors but was not cast out. My white friends joked with me and celebrated my new identity albeit in a racist way. The administrator, who had since moved on, would have had her suspicions confirmed. The university hadn't banished or refused me, as it would have done to students like me who were black and female only forty years before. Should I resent the bitter history of exclusion, or just be glad that the university, along with the country, had made progress? And what about all those who had endured segregation? Could my achievement and the achievement of those like them ever make up for the generations who were denied?

I felt all these things along with guilt, shame, and self-righteousness. The serene and stately beauty of the East Coast was the only location in which I had really pictured living. New York–style intellectualism was the only model I had, and I was taught that there was none better. Even though by the end of my graduate studies I had traveled throughout Russia, Europe, and a bit in Asia, I couldn't imagine life, especially the kind of life I wanted to have, in any other part of the country. I supposed my preference for overcast, rainy skies and my belief that they alone cultivated the mind had influenced my choices for travel and study.

In high school, I was a proud regionalist, asking with rhetorical sarcasm, "How can anyone think or study when it's always sunny? It's just not an intellectual climate."

I didn't know there was inherent racism in that statement, the kind that led proponents of environmental determinism in the nineteenth century to believe that the tropical climates of the Southern Hemisphere led the people of those regions to be uncivilized, lazy, promiscuous, and overall degenerate while the bracing weather of Northern Europe encouraged the stronger work ethic, intelligence, and civilized behavior of the superior race.

These notions weighed upon me more because I was about to leave the East Coast. I had been accepted into a Mellon postdoctoral program for the humanities at the University of California–Los Angeles, beginning the following autumn. When I told Professor

Savich the good news of my acceptance and that I had been selected for the position by the faculty of UCLA's Slavic department, he snorted, "I'm surprised they chose you; it's a very patriarchal department."

Earlier that same year at our national conference, I was following up with a faculty member from another university on a question I'd asked during a panel. Savich, who had attended the panel as well, joined us to interject, "I see you've met Sarah. She always speaks her mind."

I'd taken it as a compliment at the time. I thought scholars were supposed to engage in critical debate. Later, I came to realize he was implying that I didn't know my place. *Screw him*, I thought. I'd taken pleasure in proving Ivor Savich wrong when he'd underestimated me in the past, as when I applied for an interdisciplinary fellowship at Princeton's Center for the Study of Religion. The project was funded through the Templeton Foundation; it was a big deal. When I asked Professor Savich to look over my proposal, he conceded that the topic was ambitious and intriguing but would never be accepted by the center's director, who was a well-known professor on the sociology of religion.

"I applied for a similar project, and he rejected my application," he said. "He's a sociologist and doesn't understand literature." I submitted the proposal and the project was accepted.

Despite Professor Savich's skepticism of my abilities, I had looked up to him; he epitomized the kind of intellectual I aspired to be. Harvard educated, he was the leading authority in his field. His work was respected, and although our personalities clashed, I admired his meticulous, insightful scholarship. But I realized I was glad to be leaving the circumscribed world over which he and others like him lorded. As I thought about Los Angeles, which may as well have been

Mars, I started to picture new possibilities for myself. Since high school I had been programmed to shoot for the Ivy League. Maybe, I thought, there was more out there for someone like me. Later that week, I packed my suitcases, sold my futon, and said goodbye to my housemate.

Michael was a professor at the University of California–Riverside and already lived in Los Angeles. My moving there felt like destiny. We'd lived together for a few months in Princeton, but in Los Angeles, I wanted my own place; I wanted a chance to discover the city for myself.

Twenty-nine

Warm sun, bright flowers, beautiful people—Los Angeles was a city of dreams, energy, possibility. The entire landscape of my world changed. The Tudor, brick, and stone of the East Coast transformed into terra-cotta, whitewashed stucco, and red-tiled roofs. Maples and pines became palm trees and succulents. Muggy, humid summers became a fierce dry heat. Gray skies became a cloudless blue.

Here, Asians, Latinos, and other brown folks were the majority. Each neighborhood felt like a different country that I could visit without a passport. Los Angeles was the whole world, and I felt at home in it. Leaving my family back home, the East Coast and the Ivy League behind, I finally felt like I could breathe. I found an apartment on Westside Rentals, one bedroom in a small two-story building with a nosy landlord. It was on the edge of the Fairfax District adjacent to West Hollywood, a stone's throw from the Grove, CBS Studios, and Little Ethiopia.

My academic world changed. Princeton's campus was small, centralized, and built in the style of the collegiate Gothic of Oxford and Cambridge. A tall wrought-iron structure, the infamous FitzRandolph Gate, stood between the campus and the town's main street, providing a physical and symbolic barrier, setting the school apart from—and perhaps above—those who had not gained admission. When I had arrived on campus as a wide-eyed first-year graduate student, those gates felt like a portal into an exciting and select world of the best artists, philosophers, and scientific minds the world had to offer. By the time I left six years later, beleaguered and nearly broken, the thick iron bars reaching skyward, the imposing columns of sculpted stone crowned with predatory eagles, and the elaborate spiky iron filigree surrounding the school's crest seemed like the entrance to a Gothic prison, the inscription reading "Abandon All Hope Ye Who Enter Here."

By contrast, UCLA was a sprawling metropolis of two hundred buildings and over four hundred acres. It had its own zip code. The main buildings on the quad were cathedral-like structures of red brick and tan limestone. Their ornate columns, mosaicked ceilings, and arches seemed transported from Southern Italy, bringing with them the warmth and light of the Mediterranean. I knew enough of architectural bombast by the time I arrived on campus to be wary of the idealism and superiority the place evoked, but its majesty still overwhelmed, the more modern buildings hiding around the behemoths intrigued, and I could not help drawing my hand through the hypnotic downward flow of the Inverted Fountain.

I was happily surprised when I met the other incoming fellows. Three of us had corresponded by email shortly after arriving in Los Angeles and had decided to meet up for drinks in Westwood. When we met at Westwood Brewing Company, UCLA's watering hole, we all laughed: East Coast transplants as we were, on the bright and sunny LA day, in a sea of pastel tank tops, Daisy Dukes, cargo shorts, and UGGs, we were all wearing black.

All of us were either biracial, bilingual, bicontinental, binational, bicultural, or a combination of all five. Not only were we racially and/or ethnically different from most scholars in our fields, our scholarship was interdisciplinary, going beyond or outside of what was considered the normal purviews of our respective fields. There had been no requirement for minority status on the application; in this case, it happened that the best scholars for the program were non-white.

We dubbed ourselves the Island of Misfit Toys. I ate my basket of fries and exclaimed, "Wow, even the bar food is really good in LA!" I realized what a relief it was not to feel like an outsider, or rather to have my outsider-ness validated by being chosen to be part of this select group.

When we finally met the cohort of fellows from the previous year, it reinforced what a special gathering it was; I was the only American-born fellow. Sicilian, Catalan, Afro-Canadian-Indian, Punjabi, and Egyptian German, were some of the identities I learned went with the faces of my new peers. We came from all different fields, and queer, feminist, and minority perspectives dominated our work. For the first time in my studies, none of my fellows were white Americans.

Our program directors were both women: one Taiwanese, who studied Chinese modernisms, the other ethnic French from Mauritius, who studied francophone African literature. They had coedited a collection titled *Minor Transnationalism*, which discussed how language, art, and culture around the world was enriched and driven not by mainstream or majority populations, but by immigrants and minorities who brought with them new and varied influences.

Being able to wield the knowledge of Frantz Fanon, Audre Lorde,

Edward Said, and Gayatri Spivak in my own work felt like scholarly activism. During my graduate studies, I did not read the work of postcolonial thinkers. I didn't know that kind of work existed. Now I discovered that a small number of scholars in my field were branching out to bring the discipline of Russian literature, which strictly dialogued with itself, into a more global conversation.

I spent years writing about Gennady Aygi, a poet from the small Asiatic country of Chuvashia, which was part of the Soviet Union. He was from what Russians considered a backwater, but he wrote poetry that recalled the modernists of the 1920s. He considered himself a citizen of the world. I resonated with the mix of opposites he seemed to embody. No one could pin down his identity. If he were a minority, why did he write as if he were the equal of the great Russian poets? Where were the paeans to village life? Where was the folksiness?

Critics suspected his language was experimental and "difficult" because he didn't speak Russian well. His poetry was not a work of genius but an accident caused by his ignorance. I knew what it felt like to be indefinable, to be expected to fit into one box or another, and how confused others were when I did not. I knew what it was like to have my intellect doubted despite evidence to the contrary. In grad school, when I told others I studied Russian literature, they asked if I spoke Russian. Even though the subject was obscure and, to some, exotic, no one asked that question of my white colleagues. It was as if they didn't expect someone who looked like me to be interested or competent in such a field. Even on a job interview, one of the professors, in seeming exasperation, asked, "Why do you even study Soviet literature? You weren't even born then."

His comment revealed his prejudices against someone he perceived to be too young for the subject she studied, and who, as African

American, he perceived to have no connection with the culture. I wanted to ask him why people studied Shakespeare or medieval literature. There was usually no assumption that a subject needed to correspond directly with a person's demographics, but in the case of people of color, that wasn't true. Perhaps he wanted to ask me why I studied Soviet literature and not African American literature. He seemed to wonder what possible relevance Soviet literature could have to someone like me, and what insight someone like me could possibly bring to the conversation.

Now, as I encountered the perspectives of postcolonial thinkers who laid out in great detail why the artistic work of minorities all over the world was valuable and unique, I realized that assumptions about minorities' intellectual inferiority had been around for centuries. I thought back to the pan-African graduation ceremony when I wondered what I shared with everyone else in the auditorium, and I realized it was this: our achievements would be considered inferior even when they met or exceeded the standards of achievement set out by our society. People spoke of raising and lowering the bar, but I realized there was no bar, the raising or lowering of standards was arbitrary, and often depended on how they are looked at.

To proceed to the doctoral phase of my program, students had to pass a master's exam. Our professors determined the questions on the exam, and they changed from year to year. I remembered binders thick as telephone books, study guides written by students from years past. There was no earthly way each of us could amass the necessary material on our own, so we researched the guides in minute detail, adding dozens of pages of our own to fill in the gaps.

There were no letter grades on the exam, no numerical point total, no standard means of evaluation. The goal was to achieve as close to perfection as possible, and the committee of professors decided what that meant. Looking back, the process was much more subjective than I'd realized. There were horror stories, passed down like urban legends, of grad students who failed the exam and were ousted from the program with only the dreaded credential of master's in Russian literature. That degree was a well-known code in our field for those who were not deemed fit to continue in their doctoral program. No graduate program would take them after that, and one was even less employable with that degree than with the Ph.D. we'd risked life and limb to attain.

The further I got from that environment, the more I realized how contingent my success—and the success of all students in my program—had been.

When I arrived in Princeton, I was fresh off an apprenticeship in traditional Japanese pottery at the home studio of a potter who lived in the woods of Virginia. The potter was an American who'd traveled to Japan and learned her craft in the 1960s. Her style of wearing bandannas as neckerchiefs and headbands and her aversion to wearing bras had rubbed off on me. Since I had been living in Philadelphia the year before, I had also developed the habit of detaching the front tire of my bike before locking it on the street.

I arrived on Princeton's campus braless with my curly hair tied up in a bandanna, carrying a bike tire, my car trunk full of anagama pottery like it was the most natural thing in the world. My professors must have been horrified. Perhaps, like Dean Heermance back in 1930, they thought, *Whom did we admit to our esteemed program?* I received backhanded comments from them, like being called a "free spirit." My command of Russian and the fact of my being admitted as only one of two students that year seemed to take a back seat in their evaluation of me to my unconventional appearance.

For my dissertation defense, my hair was straight, and I wore an Ann Taylor outfit with low-heeled shoes. It wasn't only scholarship, knowledge, or passion that was important; I learned that I had to conform to a certain image of what an intellectual looked like. Many of my professors looked bizarre and unkempt themselves; Professor Savich had long, bushy eyebrows and sometimes wore baggy sweaters with holes in them. Another professor wore green galoshes nearly every day and pants that looked like jodhpurs. Her face was free of makeup except for bold red or pink lipstick. Yet another professor wore her hair in a messy topknot and wore layers of baggy skirts. Their eccentricity was acceptable, but mine was not. For young scholars to be taken seriously in our field, and perhaps for me more so, conformity was half the battle.

Once, I expressed frustration to my advisor because I was not getting job interviews after attending a conference. She ventured, "Maybe you should try dressing a little more . . . conventionally."

I was wearing a head wrap, hoodie, and camo cargo pants as I sat in her office that day, but at the conference, I had worn a prim sweater with my initials monogrammed on the breast and tasteful wide-leg trousers. She did not know that because she had not attended my panel, but her comments seemed to apply to my general appearance as well as how she assumed I dressed at conferences. My advisor dressed in a more traditionally professorial manner than some of the other faculty in our department, but it didn't seem fair that there was a double standard. The other grad students in my program were pressured to conform in their style, too, but from what they told me, none of them received the freighted comments I did.

In Los Angeles, even in academia, there was far less of an expectation of conformity to white culture, thinking, and style. My directors and peers looked professional, but not at the expense of their individuality. Instead of ending our seminars with a plate of cheese and crackers, or nothing, we ended with dinner at an Italian, Iranian, or Taiwanese restaurant. There was wine and laughter. Our post-doctoral conferences were convivial and catered, with more on the table than a lone pitcher of water.

Having such festivities made us feel like we were valued by our program and university. The Mellon postdoctoral program was no smaller, our fields of research no less specialized than my graduate program, and yet we were made to feel like we were doing important work, like we belonged. When I met new people, I didn't have to pretend I was someone I wasn't. It was becoming clear to me that there was more than one way to be a scholar, and the more I realized how free I felt in LA, the clearer it became how restricted I'd felt back home.

Thirty

Not long after I moved to LA, I began seeing a therapist. My state of mind consisted of overanalyzing my mother's actions to the point of obsession, which resulted in constant frustration, and of being angry with myself, which, despite my positive experiences at UCLA, led to a steady erosion of self-confidence.

None of my colleagues knew what was going on with me; I kept this side of my personal life private. I was enjoying my new academic milieu and the friends I was making too much to complicate things with my messy personal story and worsening psychological state. To them, I was a self-confident activist scholar, easygoing, and sociable.

At home, a different side of me emerged. I was obsessive, irritable, anxious, depressed. Absorbed in an unwinnable argument and the desire to discover a truth that may or may not have been there to find. Michael was the only one who knew what I was going through. He believed I had a right to know the truth that existed behind my mother's vague and evasive account.

My mother made it clear that she had said everything she had to say on the subject of "the donor" and had given me as much information as she knew.

"Why are you lying to me?" I'd yell over the phone as the argument got heated. "Why can't you just tell me the truth?"

"Real life isn't like a book," she'd snap back, mocking my field of study. "I've told you the truth. There's no hidden love story, no matter how much you want there to be."

Through my anger, I knew there was truth to what she was saying, but I just couldn't accept it. Something wasn't right. She was still holding something back. How could I tell? She was overly defensive, it seemed, every time I brought up the subject, which was basically every time we spoke. Was she just exasperated at my insistence on revisiting something she considered ancient history? Was it trauma that never went away? Or was it something else?

I thought back to that night at the Residence Inn when I had been too sad and stunned to pick up on everything that was being yelled back and forth between my parents. I wished to God I had heard the name my father ventured because it elicited an enraged response. *The lady doth protest too much, methinks.* But then, was I just grafting a literary trope onto real life? I was no psychologist, though I considered myself fairly expert on the work of Dostoevsky. Didn't actions in real life, as in novels, have subtext? Didn't people, like characters in a well-constructed novel, betray themselves by what they refused to say?

"No, it couldn't have happened like that," my therapist, an African American woman named Dr. Wade, said after I told her my mother's story of rape. "A black man raping a white woman on a small, white campus in rural Pennsylvania in the 1970s? No," she said. "Black men have been killed for less."

Tara, Courtney, Sveta, Angie, David, and Michael were skeptical of my mother's story, too, because there were so few details, and the details she did give smacked of cliché.

"I'll never understand your mother," Tara said across a large mahogany table on one of her trips to Princeton before I graduated. We had a ritual of holding our conversations in one of the empty, ornate seminar rooms on the first floor of my building. We called these sessions the Meeting of the Minds.

"I don't know what to do," I replied, my voice echoing off the carved walls and ceiling. "Why won't she tell me the truth? Do you think she has some kind of mental illness or personality disorder? You've known my mom for years. What do you think?"

"Your mother is a mystery. There's probably some type of mental illness in the picture, but I don't know which."

When I was in high school, my mother had some health issues she thought were symptoms of heart disease. She went to the hospital and was tested for everything that could reveal a heart condition, but all tests came back negative. The doctor told her the symptoms—chest pains, heart palpitations, and shortness of breath—were most likely due to anxiety. According to my father, who accompanied her on the trip, she yelled at the doctors and told them that they were wrong: she had a heart condition and she knew it. Why weren't they taking her seriously? The doctors suggested keeping her on a seventy-two-hour psychiatric hold, but she didn't want to hear about it.

"I don't want someone's opinion on my mental health," she said.

On my father's insistence, she met with a therapist, but walked out of the session before the fifty minutes were up.

"He was an idiot," she said.

When I told Michael about this incident and about her refusal to give more details about what happened to her that night in college, he said, "Something did happen to her, but she's also hiding something."

I wanted to believe my mother even though my closest friends fueled my doubt, but I also wanted her to tell me the whole truth.

Dr. Wade was the same age as my mother. Her extended family consisted of white, black, Asian, and mixed-race individuals. Personally and professionally, she knew about the dynamics of interracial families and how children of different races were socialized differently. She also knew that whiteness was the most fragile and insecure identity.

"Whiteness makes people hide," she said during one of our sessions, "because in confronting their privilege, they have a lot to lose."

She explained the concept of white privilege, how whiteness historically protected itself and the advantages it enjoyed from the encroachment of other races. She explained the perceived dangers of miscegenation that were deeply rooted in our society, that at one time in our history, people like me were illegal, evidence of an illicit union.

She refused to diagnose my mother.

"Stay in your square," she told me.

In her view, my most immediate need was sorting out the identity transformations I was experiencing that caused my psychological anguish. Because I was raised white and socialized like a white child, I internalized white identity. Now, as I discovered my biracial and black identities, I was like a child learning who she is in the world for the first time but with an adult's mind-set and expectations. Because I was also waking up to the ways I was complicit in whiteness and how whiteness operates as an oppressive identity, I was experiencing intellectual and emotional dissolution. This identity formation and disintegration all happening at once, my therapist assured me, was something she had never seen before and could cause severe enough strain to precipitate a mental breakdown. I felt like I was on the verge.

She gave me reading on identity formation for white, mixed-race, and black individuals so I could see how each was socialized differently and progressed through their journeys of self-awareness. She emphasized that the stages of identity development occur at different times for different people; they don't all take place during childhood or the years that are typically considered the time people come of age. Adults experienced these changes, too, and no model could fully encompass how an individual experiences their sense of self.

Nevertheless, I needed guidelines and explanations, something no one up to that point had been able to give me. If I could process the changes I was undergoing intellectually, I hoped it would make the emotional turmoil easier to work through.

The theory of white racial identity development (no source was given for this theory) progressed through five stages: *unidentified identity, acceptance, disintegration, redefinition*, and *integration*. In the unidentified or naïve stage, the white person has no awareness of race or racism. They are unaware of themselves as racial beings and may have little contact with people of other ethnicities, leading to negative stereotypes. During acceptance, a person cognitively examines and acknowledges their state of being white. At this stage, white people either avoid contact with minorities or develop a patronizing attitude toward them. They do not yet acknowledge the existence of racism. In disintegration, a white person blames the dominant group as a source of racial inequality rather than blaming the minorities themselves. The white individual becomes aware of their own racial biases and becomes angry, hurt, and pained, with these feelings directed at themselves and their own racial group. In the fourth stage, redefinition, the white individual begins to confront their biases, rejects paternalism, and accepts minorities as intellectual equals. Integration or autonomy arrives when the white person realizes how they have benefited in society from being white and how whiteness has negatively impacted people of color. The white person develops an actively nonracist identity and works to help eradicate oppression and racism.

The theory of black racial identity formation (Cross) comprised five stages: *pre-encounter, encounter, immersion, internalization,* and *commitment.* During pre-encounter, the black individual has internalized a neutral or negative attitude toward blackness. They consider race as only a problem or stigma and are socialized to favor a Euro-centric perspective. During the encounter phase, the black individual experiences an event that forces them to confront how blackness and racism impact their lives. It forces the individual out of their comfort zone and leads to confusion, anxiety, and depression. In immersion, the black person chooses clothing, hairstyles, and politics that defy Eurocentric culture and has a dichotomous view of the world: everything is either black or white. In this stage, black people feel both rage and pride. Internalization leads a black person to establish relationships across racial lines with those who are respectful and acknowledge their self-definition. A person expresses the desire to form coalitions even as they maintain a strong love for and acceptance of African American communities. When they reach the stage of commitment, black individuals become self-determining, whether it means suspending political action for other pursuits or dedicating themselves to furthering the cause of blackness.

The theory of biracial identity formation (Henriksen) identifies six stages: *neutrality, acceptance, awareness, experimentation, transition,* and *recognition.* When a person is neutral in relation to biracial identity, they do not acknowledge being different in any way. They block out whispers, stares, and other energy that suggests there is something different about them. They may feel uncomfortable but do not pursue the cause of these feelings. During the second stage, the biracial person accepts the identity society has given them. The person does not ask questions because what everyone else thinks must be correct. The individual may still have a sense that something is off but quickly dismisses those feelings and returns to daily life.

When a biracial person becomes aware of being different, a flood of anxiety is unleashed; they feel a great need for self-examination. They feel lonely and abandoned, wondering in which ways they are like one group and in which ways they are like the other. If society has placed negative stereotypes upon each group, how do you identify with them? Dread and depression at this stage heighten as pressure mounts to make a decision. In the experimentation phase, biracial people decide to emulate or join the group in which they feel most comfortable. This can also lead to depression because they risk rejection by others who don't think they belong. At this point, a biracial person can suffer from a dissociative physical and emotional state. During the transition period, a biracial person remains distant from both groups, creating a circle of chosen family and friends that do not share the racial characteristic of either side of their family tree. This could lead them to feel false or inauthentic. When a biracial person achieves the stage of recognition, they accept their identity as biracial but also accept both sides of their biological family tree. They no longer experience the internal conflict of feeling the need to choose between identities and become comfortable in their own skin.

Reading through the stages of racial identity formation blew my mind. I saw how clearly my life experience from childhood followed the biracial identity model even though I didn't realize it at the time;

I saw how I'd struggled to let go of my anti-black prejudices and felt betrayed and angry with white people and myself for being the architects and beneficiaries of racism.

Dr. Wade encouraged me to read up on biracial identity and to find a spiritual practice that would help center me and give me hope, which was something I lacked.

She framed the story I'd been told about my biological father from the perspective of a young black man in a remote, white town, probably the first in his family to attend college. It was the first time I heard the story from his side. She suggested that dating an African American was an adventure for my small-town, conservatively raised mother. Then, when things went too far, she got scared, realized she didn't want a life of shame and ridicule for being with a black man, and married my father, who was the safer choice.

All this sounded plausible and implied that my mother knew or suspected that she wasn't pregnant with my father's child but told him that she was.

Dr. Wade assured me that even if it were true that my parents conspired in a lie and my mother wasn't being truthful about her past, I needed to focus on my own growth and development. Trying to unravel that messy web would eat up all my energy and lead to a psychological collapse. She gave me a small, leather-bound book called *The Impersonal Life*.

"Focus inward and listen to the small voice inside yourself," she said. "It will tell you the truth."

Thirty-one

I tried to follow Dr. Wade's advice, but I was still too fixated on my doubts and suspicions. Inside, I was a ball of confusion, anger, and doubt. My mother and I were locked in opposite perspectives; every time we talked on the phone and I pressed the issue of my father with her, she insisted that it didn't matter and that I was throwing a tantrum like a child because she refused to give me what I wanted. I felt that she had betrayed me by withholding the truth for so long and now I could not trust anything she said. We were hurt by the other's actions and couldn't move past it.

"You can choose how things affect you," she'd say. "Don't label yourself or let others define you." She didn't seem to realize that for most of my life, she'd both labeled and defined me. The subtext of her remarks was that I should not let being African American, which to her was nothing more than a set of stigmas, define who I was.

Michael was the only model I had for someone who had integrated his biracial and multicultural identity. He was comfortable with his English and Igbo heritage, even though his mixed features often led other Igbos to misidentify him. He was comfortable in Nigerian, British, and American society. He spoke English, Igbo, and some Yoruba. Wherever he traveled to his literary readings and festivals, be it in Thailand, South Africa, or Italy, he could always connect with the locals. He was someone who owned his multifaceted identity in a way I could only imagine.

In the spring of 2008, Michael and I traveled to Turtle Beach, Jamaica, for the Calabash International Literary Festival, where he had been invited to perform. We stayed in a stucco cottage on the beach, windows open to the sea air. He'd arranged for me to have a massage at the hotel's open-air spa, and as I walked back, the afternoon sun turning to dusk, I heard the sounds of his saxophone coming from the roof deck. As I walked up the stairs, I saw they were strewn with rose petals and candles. When I reached the top, he finished his serenade, then got down on one knee. He presented a diamond ring and asked me to marry him. I knelt down in front of him, threw my arms around him, and said yes.

I felt like I was beginning a new life with someone who understood all of me, not just the parts that were acceptable or easy. He recognized my complexities because he embodied them, too; as a writer who was of mixed race, he understood the ambiguities of identity and the difficulty others had in placing him—a black man in academia who knew his white colleagues were suspicious of or hostile toward his presence among their ranks. Michael knew what it was like to have a mother who, despite loving her mixed children, still harbored the deep-seated racism of her upbringing. He made it through his experiences of trauma to become a loving, graceful, creative person. He could hold all of me and I him.

I called my parents from the hotel's patio café to tell them the news. My father was happy for me. My fiancé had called him in advance and asked him for his permission, without my knowing. I appreciated the gesture of respect, and I knew my father did.

He put my mother on the phone, and her tone was much different. Her voice was full of worry. She liked Michael, she insisted, but she wanted me to be sure marriage was what I wanted.

I just wanted her to be happy for me. Michael and I had dated for three years, and my parents had met him in Princeton and when we came home to Wexford together for holidays. Michael was sure they both liked him but remarked that, as with most white Americans he'd met, they didn't quite know how to place him, and because of that, they were slightly uncomfortable. My mother asked him a lot of personal questions, and he was happy to answer. But she worried that I considered him a mentor, someone whose advice I took over hers. This was true. He was older and wiser than me, and I respected his experience. I had not taken my mother's advice about anything for a long time, and she felt like my fiancé was her replacement. I was sure Freud would have a lot to say about that.

Michael and I had moved in together in the fall, and when we returned to LA, we painted the apartment in Caribbean shades of blue and green. I began hunting down addresses of family members to invite them to the wedding that we planned for the following summer.

Among those most difficult to locate was my godfather, Jimmy. He grew up in the same small town as my mother and went to college with my father at West Virginia University. Jimmy had many friends at the college my mother attended, and he brought my dad along on one of his trips, which is how my parents met. Jimmy was practically a part of the family when I was growing up. He and my aunt Liane, my mother's older sister, were my godparents.

While not a blood relative, he was a constant fixture in my childhood and one of my biggest supporters when I played basketball in high school. But he never seemed to have a steady job. He had driven a taxi in New York, worked as a caddy for the golf course my dad played at, and sometimes painted houses. He lived with us for a while when I was little. He was a man of contradictions. We never knew what he was doing or where he was going next. As I got older, he became more and more distant from our family, until we finally lost touch.

After playing phone tag and having emails bounce back from his full in-box, I resorted to snail mail, writing Jimmy a letter to let him know I was getting married in California and wanted him to be there.

I took the opportunity to tell him about the secret that my parents revealed about my paternity. Since he knew my parents better than anyone back then, I asked him for information about who my father might be. I was moving forward with my life, maybe even starting a family, and I didn't want to do that while I was missing such an important piece of my own history.

A few weeks later, I received a reply written in a blocky, uneven hand.

Jimmy congratulated me on my upcoming wedding and ended his letter with the line:

If you really want to dig up the past I can tell you.

Finally, I thought, someone was willing to tell me the truth about what happened. If that were the case, though, why end the letter with just a teaser? Was he giving me a chance to back out, to be absolutely sure I wanted to venture down that path?

I wrote him an enthusiastic letter back saying, yes, I absolutely wanted—needed—to know what happened back then.

He left me a phone message saying he was happy to hear from me and would be at my wedding, "even if it were in Japan." But he didn't mention the events about which he promised to tell me. I wondered if he had talked to my parents and been dissuaded from pursuing the matter.

His evasiveness led me to formulate wild plots. Maybe he and my parents were involved in a crime—a murder? Why did he say *dig up the past*? Why use those words? Was there something they were all complicit in and wanted to keep quiet?

I told Michael about these suspicions, and he quelled them.

"If that were the case, they wouldn't have told you at all; they would have kept lying."

For the moment, I abandoned my conjectures and dove into wedding planning full force.

My girlfriends from the postdoctoral program went dress shopping with me at Saks Fifth Avenue in Beverly Hills. We had a champagne brunch in the rooftop café overlooking the bustle of Wilshire. I felt I were living the kind of life I had only ever dreamed about. I was engaged to the love of my life in a fantastic city on the brink of a successful career and a whole new sense of self. It felt like a second chance.

Thirty-two

On June 20, 2009, Michael and I married in a nondenominational ceremony on the rooftop of the Canary Hotel in Santa Barbara, California.

Thanks to bridal boot camp, I looked tanned and toned in my gauzy Vera Wang gown. Tara, Courtney, and Amy—to whom I grew closer as I lost touch with Abby—were my bridesmaids and attended to me as if I were a queen. Tara, my maid of honor, agreed to intervene with my mother if she decided to make trouble during the wedding.

My gown was strapless, the bodice covered in delicate layers of chiffon with an empire waist that blossomed into billowing skirts of chiffon and silk, perfect for a beachside wedding. My hair and veil were short, and I wore vintage-inspired accessories. The ring my fiancé had picked out for me was a square-cut canary diamond framed by slim white baguettes. He'd made sure to buy it from a retailer that sourced diamonds ethically. As a West African, he knew the savageries of the industry went beyond what Hollywood portrayed in *Blood Diamond*.

We saw the movie at the Grove, and on the way back to the car, I faltered in disbelief.

"Yes," Michael said, "it is really like that, only much worse and with no fairy-tale ending."

My bridesmaids wore short pearl-gray silk dresses in the same empire cut as my gown, and the color accented their pale skin and dark blond hair perfectly. Next to my warm-toned darker skin, black hair, and ivory gown, they looked like the perfect ladies-in-waiting.

The theme was tropical. My bouquet overflowed with fuchsia orchids. The aisle was strewn with bright pink and orange petals. The tables were adorned with white candles and tropical flowers. My mother seemed happy, even excited. She got her hair done with the bridesmaids and me. The photographer snapped some touching photos of her affixing a bracelet to my wrist while she smiled wistfully.

A British friend of Michael's—a peer, no less—officiated our ceremony. It was the eve of the summer solstice, and the town transformed into a festival ground. Colored streamers sailed through the streets while figures on stilts wearing tall papier-mâché masks danced in the parade.

My father walked me down the aisle. He was emotional; I don't know if he ever thought the day would come. Maybe no father does. I know that the moment, for him, was bittersweet.

A classical violinist friend of Michael's accompanied my walk down the aisle with a piece he had written specially for the ceremony.

Kate, Michael's younger sister, was his best man, and two writer friends, one white, one African American, were his groomsmen.

I beamed as I stepped out from behind the trellis heavy with bougainvillea and caught my soon-to-be-husband's gaze. He hadn't seen me in the dress, and his eyes were bemused and misty. The collective "Aah" that every bride wants to hear rose from the audience.

Michael and I wanted to incorporate Igbo tradition into the ceremony. Both of Michael's parents had passed away, and the only family members who attended the wedding were two of his three brothers, Albert and James, and Kate.

Before we said our vows, Michael's older brother, Albert, stepped forward to present to my father a bottle of scotch to symbolize goodwill between our families. Then he turned to me and asked, "Where is your husband?"

I had to symbolically look around the crowd for my husband, though he was standing beside me. When I pointed to him as if I were surprised, it broke the tension, and the guests laughed.

At the reception, we had Caribbean food and a Nigerian DJ. Our first dance was to Buena Vista Social Club's "Chan Chan."

Albert and James led the room in an Igbo kola nut ceremony and a call-and-response ritual to get the guests excited to kick off the reception. One of our professor friends from Riverside, who was African American, leaned over to his tablemate and said, "Now that is culture."

The lights darkened, and we showed a slideshow of Michael and me, who grew up in different decades in different parts of the world, in side-by-side photos starting with each of us as infants, then children, teens, and eventually adults. Michael's close friends Ron and Beth, who were like surrogate parents to him, stood in for him as guardians at the ceremony. They sat with my paternal grandparents at one of the tables nearest the slideshow.

"How wonderful that these two biracial people from different continents found each other," Beth said.

My grandfather "corrected" her, "No, Sarah isn't biracial. We have Cossacks in our family."

In the days after the wedding, Beth relayed this to my husband.

"It was so absurd, Beth didn't know what to say!" Michael told me.

We both had a good laugh. This was a justification even I hadn't heard before. Maybe my dad's father had been telling people all along that his granddaughter was the product of Cossack blood. It certainly added insight to my interest in Russia, and perhaps because of that, my grandfather reverse-engineered the connection. Cossacks had a reputation for being swarthy, wild folk, with large mustaches and tall hats that gave them a Eurasian look, but they were actually ethnic Russians. I've been asked before if I were Russian, since it's usually the only connection people can fathom for why I studied Russian literature.

"You look like a foundling from the Caucasus," a white friend of Michael's said to me when I first met him. I wondered if he even knew what anyone from the Caucasus region—Georgians, Abkzhazians, or Chechens—looked like. I had recently learned about Afro-Abkhazians, a diasporic group that lived in Abkhazia between the seventeenth and nineteenth centuries, making them literal African Caucasians.

But I didn't think Michael's friend or my grandfather knew these histories. The labels *Cossack* and *Caucasus* signaled that I was far enough from white to be exotic but not far enough to be black. I expected this kind of rationalization from a stranger; presumptions about my exotic roots had dogged me since I was a child. But it was a surprise—and a sad one after I got over the initial hilarity—that such an excuse had come from my own grandfather on my wedding day.

My aunts, uncles, and cousins on my father's side of the family, I

found out later, all knew or suspected that I was not biologically related to them. My grandfather must have known, too. The side-by-
side photos of my husband and me as children showed that we shared
a similar ethnic mix: he English and Igbo, and I Italian and African
American. It was probably clear to everyone in the room that we were
both of mixed African and European heritages. We had the same
look. Only the people closest to me, my family, chose not to see it.

Thirty-three

My first year of marriage was difficult.

We were married in June 2009, but that same month, my post-doctoral program that had given me a sense of belonging and renewal ended. Most of the friends I made in the two-year program went off to separate corners of the world to pursue the next phases of their careers. We all wanted assistant professorships on the tenure track, which these days were only available when an emeritus professor retired or died. Because tenure guaranteed lifelong employment, professors usually remained in their positions long after the standard retirement age of sixty-five. In some sense, this was understandable because it could take almost that long to reach the rank of full professor. Tenure-track job openings were few, and successful candidates had to move to wherever the job was rather than picking a place they wanted to live and looking for a job there.

In 2009, the country was undergoing an economic recession. My friends left LA, and I saw businesses disappear from Wilshire and Fairfax, leaving empty storefronts in their wake. No one walked in LA, but the streets felt subdued, the sidewalks deserted.

Michael continued his schedule of continuous travel for readings and speaking gigs. That fall, he was going to be the writer in residence at Northwestern University in Evanston, Illinois. He would reside there for the fall quarter, from August to December.

Unlike my postdoctoral friends, I hadn't secured a position for the next academic year. Slavic studies was a miniscule field during the best of times, and now universities were cutting funding for small departments. If a professor of Russian retired, instead of creating a job opening, the university eliminated the position.

I faced the prospect of a friendless year with no husband and no job.

"Work on your translations," Michael advised.

I was translating the Russian poems of Gennady Aygi, the Chuvash poet on whom I'd written my dissertation. I cared about the project but found it hard to focus when the stability I had built with people I loved in a city I loved was pulled out from under me.

Once Michael left in August, the bright Caribbean walls of our apartment didn't cheer me; they made me depressed. I began feeling short of breath and visited a doctor who was a family friend and a guest at our wedding. Like my mother had done years before, I made him perform a stress test and EKG reading to make sure I wasn't having a heart attack. His diagnosis was the same: anxiety.

He prescribed my first antianxiety medication. It helped phenomenally at first, but I still felt lonely and lost. In October, I flew halfway across the country to join Michael in Evanston. I didn't have a job there either, but I could work on my translations feeling like I had a temporary home.

The next year, with Michael's intervention, I got a position at the University of California–Riverside, teaching Russian and comparative literature. It was exactly the kind of position I wanted, but it was not permanent. The university could only receive funding for a one-year renewable contract, for a maximum of three years. My title would be *visiting assistant professor*. The "visiting" part hurt because I was no less qualified than my friends for a tenure-track assistant-ship and because my husband was already a full professor enjoying the privileges of tenure.

I planned to make my life in Los Angeles; I wasn't just visiting.

Thirty-four

I paused between bites of blueberry ricotta pancakes. My friend Claire and I were having brunch at BLD, and I was telling her that I had reached an impasse with my mother in finding out more about my biological father. I told her about Jimmy, my godfather, who'd offered to tell me who my father was but who then mysteriously broke contact. He never came to the wedding, emailing that he'd had a falling-out with my mother and didn't want their bad blood to spoil the event. The falling-out, he'd said, was about an old friend of my mother's he used to date.

Claire was a writer who was mixed race, with olive skin and straight hair. Most people thought she was Italian or Indian; even I could not see a trace of blackness in her features. Unlike me, she'd grown up with a strong sense of black identity. Claire's mother, who was white, made sure Claire and her siblings understood they were black and what that meant in our society. It was a political choice. Claire knew who her father was, but he was not always in her life. She, too, was writing a memoir about her search to learn more about her father, her parents' relationship, and how his identity related to her own.

She asked me a question I hadn't thought of, and it gave me pause.

I'd told her that when I'd arrived in LA, one of the first things I did was look up the website of the college my mother attended to see if they had digitized any old yearbooks. I knew the year range and thought that if my biological father graduated, I might be able to find his photo. I didn't have a name or a face to go on, but I thought I could narrow down the possibilities with online research.

When I found the website, there was one yearbook issue from every decade available online, but none of them matched the years I was looking for. Still, I scanned the pages and found that, as I'd suspected, there were few students of color. I was surprised to find that of the black students, male and female, at least half of them were African. I wondered why I'd never considered the possibility of international students at the college, maybe because it was small and rural. I'd assumed most students would be from the surrounding area in western Pennsylvania. That turned out to be true, judging by the hometowns listed under the names of each of the seniors' photos.

But it didn't matter, I told Claire, because the dates of the yearbooks I needed weren't available.

"That was three years ago," Claire said. "Why not try again?"

I argued that even if the yearbooks I needed were digitized, I had nothing to go on.

"Why don't you just look for someone who looks like you?" Claire said between forkfuls of salad.

It seemed obvious, but somehow I'd never thought of that. I was trying to get information from family, mainly my mother, and none had been forthcoming. Maybe I was the key after all. Maybe it was that simple.

When I got home, I went straight to my desktop and pulled up the website. A few more yearbooks from each decade had been digitized, and I found the years I was looking for. I scanned the senior portraits. Each featured a name, a major, and a hometown with city and state or city and country if the student was from abroad. Most students were local, from the area near the school or from cities in Pennsylvania. Seeing how many photos of black students listed hometowns in Africa, I realized the person I was looking for might be a foreign student.

For most of my life, I had been convinced that my looks were not black looks, and it was difficult for me to imagine that I would recognize my own face in a man with dark skin from thirty-odd years ago.

At the moment, I had nothing else to go on. Based on looks, I narrowed the possible suspects down to five photos. One was light skinned and wore glasses. I'd had laser eye surgery a few years before, but before that, I'd worn glasses for nearsightedness for most of my life. My vision was much worse than anyone else's in my family. Could that be a genetic clue? Was eyesight genetic? Despite the guy's large polyester collar and plaid shirt—could someone with such a poor sense of style be related to me?—I decided to put him in the "strong maybe" pile.

Most of the African and African American students didn't seem to look like me; their features were proportioned differently, faces and ears shaped differently, ears sitting at a different height, shoulders too small or too rounded. Then again, there was only so much you can tell from a 1970s senior portrait. For men and women, black and white students alike (there were few of other ethnicities), the haircuts were terrible and the fashion was worse. Faces that were supposed to be around twenty years old looked to be in their thirties and forties.

Flicked, feathered, and bowl-cut bobs, manes of brushed-out curls, and disco-ball Afros made everyone look like extras in a throwback B movie. Could I find an echo of myself among these faces?

My anxiety about not looking "black enough," coupled with the fact that everyone inherits features from both sides of the family, made it difficult for me to know what I was looking for. If I didn't know my mother, would I have been able to recognize her yearbook photo? We had the same smile, mouth, and chin shape, but our other features differed. Claire's simple suggestion was turning out to be more difficult than it seemed.

I was about to give up when I came across a photo that I'd overlooked. The young man in the photo was dark-skinned, so dark that I'd passed over him, thinking he couldn't be related to me. Then I looked closer and recognized the tilt of his head, his dark, almond-shaped eyes, his broad, square shoulders, rounded nose, tasteful attire, and most of all, the hopeful, youthful look in his eyes that reminded me of my own high school senior portrait.

With Photoshop, I removed the photo from the yearbook and superimposed upon it a photo of myself at around the same age. I didn't change any of the features in either photo. I made sure the scale and three-quarters head tilt of the photos matched. I changed the opacity on the top photo so that the photo in the layer below could be seen, like a ghost, through the other. What I saw took my breath away.

Seamlessly, my photo transformed into his, and his into mine, down to the height and width of the hairline. The shoulders matched up, the eyes, the cheekbones, the height of the ears. His nose and lips were broader than mine, but the shape was the same. Even the smile that showed his straight teeth matched. Both photos were black and white, and my light skin faded into his darker skin with all the features intact as I slid the opacity bar from right to left. We looked like a male and female version of the same person; skin color was the only difference.

I wished I could find software that mapped faces to determine shared genetic traits. Did that exist? Could I get my hands on it? I thought I'd seen it on the History or Discovery channels and *CSI*. I wondered if that software was real or just a fiction, like the montages of crime-scene laboratory work that produced instant results to assure us that science will always swiftly and unequivocally catch the criminal.

I brought Michael in to look at the results of my experiment. He was as shocked as I was; the resemblance was uncanny. He laughed. "You married an African, and it turns out you *are* African!"

The name below the photo was Gideon; major, Communications; hometown, Nairobi, Kenya.

It was a dream I dared not mention to find out that my biological father was not the villain he was painted to be. Looking through other photos in the yearbook, I saw that Gideon was on the soccer team and part of the international student organization. A broad, confident smile, good fashion sense, a student athlete with a hopeful look in his eye? Could this be the same ill-intentioned person who took advantage of my mother? Would a black foreign student at a school with a white, rural majority take that chance? It didn't seem likely, and yet her story and the photo were all I had to go on. All I wanted was to feel a connection that had been missing all my life. Now, whatever connection I found would be muddied with the possibility or reality that the man in the photograph was a rapist and I was his biological daughter.

I was determined to find out as much as I could about this person and establish the connection without doubt. Through an online search of his name, I found the British-style boarding school he had attended in Kenya and the national radio station he'd helped to build.

I thought maybe I could finally get a straight answer by emailing the photo to my parents and my mother's parents. Would they recognize him? Would they admit it if they did?

My mother denied it, saying, "I've never seen this man before in my life." My father also denied knowing him.

My grandfather's answer was more ambiguous. "I don't know who he is," he wrote, "but does he have a nickname?"

I looked in the yearbook again but couldn't find any mention of a nickname.

It occurred to me that even if my grandfather didn't know who Gideon was, he must have known of or heard about a black student involved with my mother who did have a nickname. I emailed him and asked if he could be more specific, but he only responded, "Don't be angry with your mother."

Anger wears away at you, and I was physically and mentally exhausted. I wanted our battle to be over, but our desires were too much in conflict. It was a power struggle for information but also a yearning for forgiveness, love, and acceptance. We were both mistrustful people whose feelings were easily hurt. Neither of us could handle betrayal, and it was almost impossible for us to forgive and forget as others might have been able to in the same situation.

I told Tara about the photo first. She was shocked and agreed the guy was a dead ringer for me. She also found my parents' denial suspicious.

Later, I asked Michael what he thought of my family's silence around my reveal of Gideon's photo. He responded with a German proverb: "No answer is also an answer."

Even though Gideon's photo said he was from Kenya, when I

looked up his last name to see what ethnicity he might be, most of the results came from Nigeria. Maybe I was Nigerian after all!

I wondered what truth lay behind my family's silence. Even though the resemblance between Gideon and me was striking, maybe he wasn't the guy and my parents really didn't recognize him. Or was I just trying to fool myself, afraid of what it would mean for me to have finally found the father I was looking for?

I had one clue: a nickname. A Kenyan student named Gideon would have been unique in western Pennsylvania, and maybe his American classmates preferred to call him something else.

Even though I didn't have any confirmation, I wanted this handsome, enterprising young Kenyan to be my father. I wanted my mother's story to be a lie, so for the time being, I put it out of my mind. I printed out Gideon's black-and-white photograph and put it in a frame in my study. I watched the Oscars with the framed photo nearby and kept looking, gazing at it, like I had a crush. I practiced looking at it, mentally saying, *This is my father.* It would take a while to integrate that information into my sense of self, but I needed something to hang on to. I only needed to repeat the story to myself like our family story had been repeated to me.

Thirty-five

Later that year, my grandfather on my father's side, Pop, passed away. My brother Patrick and I flew into Philadelphia from LAX, and my parents picked us up at the airport to drive down to Long Beach Island, New Jersey, for the funeral.

My father navigated the black Yukon out of the airport onto I-95. Tommy and his girlfriend, Julie, flew in from Pittsburgh and were already in the car. Julie was easygoing and self-possessed. I hoped she would not have to experience the full force of our family's insanity, but it was already beginning.

My father had probably been at the airport all day waiting for our flights, which he'd scheduled and paid for, to arrive. It was six in the evening, and we still had two more hours to go with traffic. None of us had eaten, and we were all on edge, having been brought together for this unexpected family reunion.

"What was the inciting event?" my mother was asking from the front seat as we pulled onto the interstate. After years of staying home with us, she had gone back to school and became a nurse practitioner. She wanted to know the specific medical details of my grand-father's death.

"Didn't he have a heart attack?" Patrick and I both chimed in. "That's what you told us over the phone."

"No, he had a cardiac arrest; that's different," my mother said and launched into a medical explanation of how the two differ.

The events leading up to Pop's death seemed to be: Paula, his wife, woke him when she realized he had vomited in his sleep. She called an ambulance, and Pop was well enough to step into the ambulance himself.

By the time he arrived at the hospital, which was forty miles away, most of his organs had failed and he ceded, no longer conscious.

"That doesn't seem right," my mother said. "I want to see the autopsy report. I want to know what really happened."

"Septic shock," my brother Tom ventured from the farthest row of seats. "From inhaling his own vomit."

"Kathleen said it was a hundred degrees in that house when she visited last week," my mother parried. Kathleen was my aunt, my father's youngest sister. Like my mother, Kathleen didn't like Paula.

"What are you saying?" I asked, exhausted, from the middle row. "Do you suspect foul play?"

"Basically," Tom said.

"The autopsy report was only given to Paula," my father said in an even tone with a hint of exhaustion. He had been silent for most of the drive. "By law, the doctors can only give it to her."

My mother sneered and rolled her eyes. She lowered her head and pinched the bridge of her nose like she was trying to stave off a mi-graine or the world's everlasting stupidity.

"You think Paula mismanaged his care?" I asked.

"It wouldn't be appropriate to ask her for the autopsy report, not now," my father said.

My mother gave him a look of hurt that said, *Why do you always take her side?*

As we exited the New Jersey Turnpike, I remembered the sights and smells from my childhood: the weathered shingled roofs, the salty ocean air.

Long Beach Island was a thread of sand six miles at sea and less than a mile wide. The last time I was there was three years earlier for my grandmother's funeral; she was the one I was named for. She and Pop divorced years ago, and in her final years, my father moved her from her home with my aunt to a nursing home in Wexford. She wanted to be cremated and buried on LBI. I wondered how my father felt having lost both parents.

Michael was an adult when he lost his parents, but when his mother died, he said sadly, "I'm an orphan."

We arrived at the beachfront motel, the Drifting Sands, where all the out-of-town relatives would be staying, late in the evening. The building was faded yellow with chipped white banisters and staircases lining the first and second floors. It abutted the soft, sloping dunes on which grew long stalks of seagrass fenced off by thin, dark stakes secured with rows of twisted wire that were so familiar from my youth.

Everything here was familiar: the overcast sky, the murmur and crash of the cold Atlantic waves beyond the dunes, the path at the end of the road where asphalt gave way to sand and we'd climb the small slope, past the single wooden bench that marked the entrance to the beach, and run down from the sand that was hot, soft, and deep to the cool, firm, wet sand at the water's edge. The difference was that we were no longer children.

As we got out of the car into the red August evening, my father complained about a pain in his leg, and my mother became sullen, saying, "It doesn't matter," meaning that none of her questions about the circumstances leading to my grandfather's death were answered. The pain for which I'd recently gone on prescription medication gnawed at my neck and back and was made worse by the long car ride and the stress I felt at being at the mercy of my parents' arguing. Pat, who wore a thick but groomed beard, stood with the easy up-right posture of one who meditated often. Tommy cracked ironic jokes, and Julie said she was craving Twizzlers. We had no plastic pails and shovels, no folded rainbow-colored beach chairs, no bathing suits, no beach badges. We each rolled our suitcases to the foot of the motel steps while my dad went into the office to get our room keys.

Long Beach Island was a different species of beach from those on the West Coast. Santa Monica beach was wide and flat, the ocean calm and warm. The Pacific Palisades rose along the coastline in the distance, like an idyllic landscape from a film. The water was deep-blue green, the sun yellow like a child's drawing.

Here, everything about the beach was shaded in half tones. That evening, the sand was cold and felt like sugar. Tracks from sand-pipers made the faintest imprint on the dunes, as if they were almost weightless, like tracks in newly fallen snow. There was softness in the flimsy stake fences, the shaggy dune grass. Even at night, the black of the sea and sky were more charcoal gray, more purplish blue.

Not much had changed since my childhood. Patrick and I trudged up the same small dune from the road, sand filling my flip-flops, until we reached the small peak where the dunes ended and the beach began, sloping gently down to the ocean.

The ocean was rugged and full of energy, even at dusk. Only a few couples stood around the water's edge; farther down, a family

was flying a kite. I couldn't make out their faces; they were all looking at the water. I remembered when I was little, running down to the
water with my brother carrying plastic buckets shaped like sandcastles. We slopped wet sand into the buckets, imagining the feat of
engineering we would create when we brought them back to our
blankets, carrying them gingerly back up the beach so as not to spill.
We smoothed the foundation, swept pebbles and cigarette butts out
of the way, and overturned the heavy buckets.

Once we sorted out our rooms, my father rounded my brothers,
Julie, and me up to go to a dinner hosted by Paula at the home she
and my grandfather had shared for the last fifteen years. Our family
referred to it as Pop's house or *the house on Sixteenth Street* even though
the house belonged to Paula.

"Mommy isn't coming," my dad said when we got back into the
Yukon.

Thirty-six

We were death itself as we stepped out of the hulking Yukon, six black-clad figures slanting against the sunlight.

The ride to St. Francis was silent. The New Jersey day was bright, the sun bearing down with no shade, hotter than usual for August on Long Beach Island. Our heavy black clothes stood out even more, incongruous with the day's radiance. Sweat beaded behind my sunglasses.

The church was high ceilinged with cream-colored walls and long stained-glass windows. The altar stood in the middle, and before it two columns of pews stretched back to the church's main entrance. The crucifix above the altar held the figure of a serene, white-robed Jesus, not in the agony of death but already risen.

The memorial objects were arranged on the right side of the altar, with the box containing Pop's ashes on a small white-clothed podium, large framed photographs of my young grandfather around the base. The altar was covered with floral arrangements; white roses in the shape of a heart, purple and yellow flowers in the shape of the Rotary Club's wheel logo, and more roses, lilies, and carnations.

The scene was dramatically different from my grandmother's funeral a few years before. It was a cold March morning; a single rose and photograph stood near the urn. Only a few of us dotted the pews.

Now the church was full with family members arriving from Pop's and Paula's sides to give their condolences to the receiving line in front of the altar: Paula, my aunt Kathleen, my father, his brothers Steven and John, and Paula's four daughters, Debbie, Patty, Karen, and Caroline.

My mother sat in the pew in front of me, and I could tell by her set jaw that she felt she should be part of that line.

Paula was tan and fit, with short gray hair and glasses. I expected to see her pale and weepy or fragile and distant, maybe even needing a family member's support to walk, but she was in charge as usual, even today. She wore a black pleated skirt and a short-sleeved top with white, pink, and red polka dots. Her eyes were red but clear, and before taking her place in the line, she walked around handing out small packets of tissues to other family members. She approached my mother and offered a packet, but my mother turned away, her face stony.

I reached out and took the tissues from Paula and whispered the only condolence I could give. "I'm so sorry."

After an hour, everyone took their seats.

"That looked exhausting," I said to my uncle Steven as he returned from the receiving line and sat in the pew behind me. I hadn't seen Steven in over a decade. He looked like my father but with piercing blue eyes that always seemed a little sad. He introduced me to his girlfriend, Dana, who was the only other African American in the church. I wondered if she recognized me or wondered how I was his niece with no other black people present. I wondered if she felt as alienated as I did in the sea of old white faces. Maybe she guessed I was adopted, or maybe she was counting the minutes until this whole thing was over.

The music began. To my surprise, under the priest's vestments he wore the brown cassock of a Franciscan monk and waterproof hiking sandals. I'd only attended mass led by priests who wore a black-and-white collar and black trousers below their colorful vestments. Without realizing it, I'd felt a kind of comfort in the formal, conservative appearance of the priests I knew from childhood; it echoed the spirituality and solemnity of the mass, which, despite my disagreement with most other things about the Catholic Church, I'd always respected. Father Steve wore his white hair in a buzz cut like a retired quarterback.

Looking at Father Steve and his monk's attire, it occurred to me that this was the St. Francis Parish my grandfather had been involved with since we were kids. He was always doing charity work in the church and community organizing. Every year when we were young, we would receive a T-shirt for the annual St. Francis eighteen-mile run. Standing in the pew waiting for the processional to end, I wondered if the race still went on, and if so, what color the T-shirts were this year.

When we were seated, my aunt Kathleen approached the podium to read the eulogy, my father, red-eyed, standing behind her for support. She began with a quotation from Robert Frost, who—unbeknownst to me—was one of my grandfather's favorite poets. With a breaking voice, she read from "Stopping by Woods on a Snowy Evening":

The woods are lovely, dark, and deep,
But I have promises to keep,

And miles to go before I sleep,
And miles to go before I sleep.

As many do, perhaps unconsciously, she inserted the word *lonely* for *lovely*. It seemed like a more fitting image: the poem's speaker alone at night, staring into a cold, dark forest before traveling on. It fit better with the occasion; it fit with the way we all felt at that moment.

My brother and I gave readings. I went second, and when I reached the podium, looking out into a sea of sad, mostly unfamiliar faces, I realized I was more nervous than I expected I'd be. After all, I lectured to classes of 150 students. I was used to standing in front of a crowd. But this was different. I was aware of my own difference in a roomful of people I was supposed to be related to but was not. Great-aunts and uncles I hadn't seen since I was a child looked at me as if I were a stranger. In the program, I noticed that my mother had rendered my name as *Sarah (Dunn) Valentine*, perhaps so people would remember who I was; perhaps so that I would.

After the readings and gospel, Father Steve began his homily.

"Sometimes it seems like the wood is lonely, dark, and deep, but Bob's wood was not lonely, nor was it dark or deep. His wood, his life, was full of love. Just look around." He gestured toward all of us, the pews packed even to the back row, even the section located to the side of the altar. Most of these were people from the community, other retirees who knew my grandfather as "Bob."

The priest's sentiment was sincere, but the wording sounded off. I elbowed Pat gently, eyebrows raised, and he replied by imperceptibly shaking his head and slightly rolling his eyes as if to say, *Figures*. I even heard my mother chuckle slightly in the pew in front of us. Later, in our motel room, over a bag of Twizzlers, Pat and I would talk about how the priest missed the point of the verse, misinterpreting the poet's metaphor of death, which was terrifying, unknown, but somehow still beckoning. We were much more comfortable with a literary interpretation.

"As Christians, we believe that death is not the end, but the beginning of our eternal life with God," Father Steve continued. "I believe Bob is with God now in a way we don't understand. And I believe he is there in his unique personhood. And what make a person, a life, unique, are memories—memories of family and friends. So, if you follow my Franciscan logic, because we are all in Bob's memories, a little piece of us is up there with God now, because of Bob."

This I had never thought of, that it is all these tiny moments that make a life, moments shared with the people who are most dear to you. Books, work, one's legacy or thoughts or beliefs or ideas in the abstract; the import of these is constructed afterward, mostly by people who don't know you. One way or another, nothing exists that isn't shared.

"The communion hymn is 'Here I Am, Lord,' page 412," Father Steve's voice cut in.

Here I am, Lord. Is it I, Lord? We sang.

I was overwhelmed by the tune, so familiar from my childhood, from masses I attended every Friday and Sunday in elementary school. The cantor's operatic voice soared, carrying all of us with it.

All the songs and prayers I learned in childhood I could recite to that day. As the lines formed for communion, I thought: should I go? I had not been to church, not received communion in over a decade, not counting one Christmas with my parents and my grandmother's funeral. I supposed I didn't care then, but I did now. For some reason I wanted to do what was right, as a person and as a Catholic, to honor both my grandfather's memory and the religion that the family shared. A funeral is also a celebration that the rest of us are still here, and somehow, receiving communion seemed to represent, amidst death, our continuity of life.

Pat was sitting closest to the aisle and I wonder: would he go? Like me, he hadn't had anything to do with the Church for a long time. But the people in the row in front of us were rising, and Patrick and I stood up and walked with folded hands toward the altar.

I felt there were no words for who I was, for what I felt at that moment. I was sad for all of us; sad because of sadness, sadness that is not yet loss, but our collective panic at the incomprehensibility of what has happened, of what was happening. I was my grandfather's first grandchild, the daughter of his eldest son, the older sister of Tommy and Patrick, the niece of Stevie, John, and Kathleen, the second cousin of Jimmy, Jeffery, Tommy, Kevin, and Wedge. I never thought of my identity in relation to the others in my family, and how my role in their life might be important to them. I always saw myself as autonomous, which is a lie we comfort ourselves with as we move through the world. For me, to acknowledge otherwise was too humbling, and I felt ashamed for dismissing the love and relationships of the people around me. Even if the Dunns were not biologically related to me, I wouldn't be here without them. I sniffed, unsuccessfully fighting back tears. Until then I never realized how important it was for me to not let my family see me cry.

Before the service ended, Father Steve left us with one last thought.

"Patrick Mollar brought his Eagles van today," he said, referring to the RV in the parking lot painted bright white and green, with the Eagles insignia and GO EAGLES! emblazoned on either side—a gaudy, portable cheering section. "And I know how much it would have meant to Bob to see that here today." He paused. "Even though I'm a Giants fan. I guess everyone has their faults."

An appreciative chuckle rose from the pews. The buzz cut, neoprene sandals, even the Bluetooth mic Father Steve wore in his ear to deliver the homily started to make sense. Pat leaned over and whispered, "They should have replaced the Jesus on the crucifix with Randall Cunningham or Mike Schmidt."

April 18, 1987. My dad, my brother Patrick, my grandfather, and I were at Three Rivers Stadium in Pittsburgh on the day Mike Schmidt, the third baseman for the Philadelphia Phillies, hit his five hundredth home run against the Pittsburgh Pirates. Even after steroid use became rampant, hitting five hundred home runs remained a feat most players could not match. I was nine years old, Pat was four, and my dad was thirty. My grandfather was young, too, with a full head of black hair just like my dad's that set off his light-colored eyes. We had good seats, down the third base line, midway up in the stands so we could see the whole field. My dad put my brother on his lap and explained the game to him. He made sure we got nachos, hot dogs, popcorn, and soda. I was more interested in my nachos than in the game, but even at nine I could follow football, baseball, basketball, and hockey, live or on TV. Watching and playing sports was what my family did. It was a common language we shared.

It was the top of the ninth inning, and the Phillies were losing 5–6 when Mike Schmidt stepped up to bat with two runners on base. Pittsburgh had Barry Bonds and Andy Van Slyke in the outfield, Bobby Bonilla playing third. It was a sunny day, a rarity in Pittsburgh, and we had just gotten popcorn from the vendor. Mike Schmidt made contact, and the ball sailed over left field into the stands, far above the heads of Bonilla and Bonds. We were loyal Pittsburgh fans, loyal to our city, but for my dad, who grew up in Philly, the Phillies, Eagles, and Flyers would always come first. Before I knew what happened, he was out of his seat, yelling, "Yeah! Home run! Five hundred!" The popcorn went sailing to the grimy floor as the rest of the stadium joined in the cheer as Schmidt and his teammates rounded the bases. The Phils kept their lead and won 8–6. After the game, an elderly woman sitting behind us tapped my father on the shoulder and told him admiringly that she'd never seen a dad be so nice with his kids. My dad was already beaming from the victory and the history-making moment we'd just witnessed, but this made him proudest and happiest of all.

Thirty-seven

Sitting beside my brother in a sea of pews instead of stadium seats, black suits and dresses instead of team jerseys, faces blanched with tears instead of rosy with joy, I thought about how rare it was that my dad, brother, grandfather, and I gathered to share something special. There were birthday parties and graduations, family vacations to the shore, and most recently, my wedding. But those included the whole family. Never again did the four of us share an experience like we did that day at Three Rivers Stadium. At that moment, Father Steve's buzz cut, Patrick Mollar's Eagles van, and Randall Cunningham in place of Jesus didn't seem like a joke anymore. They were something I'd shared with my brother, dad, and grandfather before I was old enough to realize how special it was.

After the service, there was a small reception in a room adjacent to the church. Trays of cold cuts, chips, potato and macaroni salads, and cookies were set out. We filled our paper plates and mostly ate in silence.

My mother set up a laptop and slide projector, which we thought was going to be a memorial to Pop's life. The slideshow did show my grandfather's life from a young man in a military uniform, to his later years as a grandfather, but she completely left out the last twenty years that he'd spent as Paula's husband. The photos only showed him with our side of the family, and with my grandmother, a woman who, while beloved by her family, had not been part of his life for many years. Paula left the room without confrontation, accompanied by her daughters. When we realized the slideshow was intended to rewrite the history of my grandfather's life to exclude Paula and reinstate the version of his life my mother wanted, we disconnected the projector to save everyone, including my mother, from further embarrassment. When I asked why she would do something so blatantly cruel and untrue, I got the response: "This is how it should have been."

The wake was held in the hall of the local fire station. The box containing my grandfather's ashes sat on a card table covered in a Philadelphia Eagles beach towel. The box was draped with a smaller towel made for the 1960 Championship Anniversary Game of the Eagles versus the Packers. To the right of the towel stood a garden gnome holding a baseball and bat. To the left of the ashes stood a Guinness glass turned upside down signaling that my grandfather had had his last drink.

Toward the end of the wake, just as we were leaving, Pat told me that cousin Jimmy, one of my dad's cousins, was talking to him about the importance of us all being family, of us all having the same blood.

"Your dad, you, your brother," he'd said to him and then paused. "Your sister—well, maybe not as far as having the same blood goes." Pat told me he said it like it wasn't new information, like it was something they'd always known.

"Wow," I said. Then, "I think he and his brothers still think of me as a Dunn, though. I mean, that's the feeling I get being here. That he's saying it's important to remember we're all Dunns."

"Yeah," Pat said. "Absolutely. The point is that we're all still family."

He told me that he had come to Long Beach Island back in February for Pop's seventy-sixth birthday. During that trip he told Kathleen that my dad wasn't my real father and that I was black. He hadn't done it out of malice; he brought the subject up, assuming that, in the five years that passed since the revelation, my dad had talked to his family about it. When Kathleen said he hadn't, Pat gave her the details.

I hadn't talked much to Kathleen on this trip yet, and I wondered if she would be upset and want me to explain. I saw her talking to my mom in a corner of the fire hall and went over to them.

"Can I talk to you for a second?" Kathleen asked.

I followed her outside, worried about what she might say.

"I want you to know that you are my heart," she said holding my hand. "You don't know how important it was for John and me when you were born." She told me that my mom was important to her, too. When she felt like no one cared about her or looked after her, my twenty-year-old mom did. She told me that my mom's example showed her how to be a mother.

We hugged. Like my cousin Jimmy, Aunt Kathleen seemed to have realized my difference all along, but the fact that we were family was more important.

As the night went on, we reminisced about our days growing up on Grove Avenue. Uncle John recalled us playing hockey in the driveway, and Pat, around four years old, saying to him, "I want to be Hextal! You always make me be Vanbiesbrouck!" We talked about the next-door neighbor's dog, Sparky, that always growled at us and deflated our footballs and basketballs if they went over the fence. Pat remembered arguing with John over whether it was the Seth Joyner or Reggie White who hit Merril Hoge so hard during a game between the Steelers and the Eagers that Merril Hoge crapped his pants; whenever the subject of someone crapping their pants came up, they would call it Merril Hoge's revenge.

"Do you remember any of that?" John asked me.

"Yeah," I said. "I remember it all."

The next morning, my family and I went to the beach, for old times' sake, before saying goodbye to the Drifting Sands and LBI. As we pulled away, I wondered how my dad felt being the eldest of the Dunn clan now that his father was gone. I wondered what my mom was doing all evening in her hotel room. After the wild night, I wondered where, if at all, I fit into this family. And now that Pop was gone, as we rode over the causeway and into the Pine Barrens, I wondered if I'd ever be back.

Thirty-eight

Three weeks after returning from Long Beach Island, I was on a plane to Heathrow for another memorial service for another father. It was the ten-year anniversary of Michael's father's death, and celebrating it was an Igbo tradition.

I was exhausted from the Dunns and still suffering from anxiety and depression. The antianxiety medication I took worked for a while, but soon self-doubt, nervousness, and paranoia would flood back, making it hard to manage daily life. I thought about how self-confident and clearheaded I used to be and wondered what had changed. Was it really just the identity crisis and family upheaval I was experiencing, or was it something more permanent?

We stayed in Croydon with Michael's sister, Kate, her husband, Bruno, and their daughter, Kelechi. Michael refused to stay with his eldest brother, John, because, he said, "Everything in his house is sticky with palm oil."

Before we left Los Angeles, Michael told me the family planned on wearing traditional Igbo outfits to the ceremony. As a wedding gift, Kate had given me a traditional Igbo outfit that I'd worn at the reception after I'd changed out of my dress. The outfit was black chiffon covered with satiny yellow heart-shaped leaves. Crystals dotted the fabric. The head wrap, called *gele*, was made out of stiff black cloth adorned with silver and gold metallic thread.

I had worn scarves and head wraps before, but the material of the gele crinkled like wrapping paper and felt stiff as a board. I did not know what to do with it, so I just wore the roomy shirt secured with the wraparound skirt and a shawl of the same fabric that draped over one shoulder. I didn't want to wear the same outfit twice, and I wasn't sure if it would be taboo to wear black to this occasion.

The next morning, we got ready for the memorial service. Kelechi, not wanting to look uncool, wore a short black-and-pink sleeveless dress rather than traditional Nigerian clothing. Kate came downstairs in a beautiful, fitted, floor-length, green-and-champagne-colored mermaid-cut top and skirt. Bruno wore a traditional white linen tunic and slacks with a black cap and pocket square to match.

Even though Michael was the one who'd told me to wear something traditional, he wore black slacks and a suit jacket with a white linen shirt. To cover the "traditional" aspect, he wore a long, beaded necklace with a beaded pouch that was part of the traditional Yoruba religion Ifá. Like many middle-class Nigerians, he and his siblings had been raised Christian. Some frowned upon traditional religions, considering them uneducated and superstitious, but practicing Ifá was something that made Michael feel closer to his culture.

I wore a burgundy ensemble with a flared head wrap that Michael and I purchased from an African dress shop in LA. I asked the woman working there if she could show me how to tie the head tie, which flared like a peacock's tail in the display window. I made detailed mental notes as she worked the magic of transforming a rectangular piece of fabric into a ruffled sculptural crown on my head.

"Did you tie that yourself?" Kate exclaimed. I nodded, not mentioning that I'd had to use half a dozen safety pins to make sure it stayed in the proper shape on my head. Kate said she did not know how to tie gele. I had to admit I felt some pride.

It was a sunny September day for the memorial service. We met up with the rest of the family members outside the Catholic church to see the programs. There had been disagreement among the siblings about whether to use separate photos of their mother and father or a photo of them together. Their parents were separated for many years before their father died, and some of the siblings, including Michael, thought it was false nostalgia to portray them as a couple.

It reminded me of the controversy over the slideshow my mother made for the gathering after Pop's funeral. Pop married Paula later in life, took up traveling to Ireland, and was very involved with her grown children. My mom and others in our family resented this new version of his life, saying he hadn't been there for his own kids and shouldn't get a do-over now.

In the end, separate photos were used for Michael's parents.

Michael's elder brothers wore traditional Nigerian shirts. Their wives were dressed like Kate, in fitted tops with capped sleeves and matching full-length, fitted skirts that flared at the knee. Even Phil, James's Irish wife, wore this kind of outfit. The two elder wives wore gele.

I glared at Michael; even though I didn't know Nigerian fashion, I could see that my outfit was different from the others: boxy, heavy fabric with large yellow satin flowers and yellow satin scalloped edges on the hems. Their dresses looked more modern, and I didn't remember seeing such ensembles—made out of traditional fabrics but with a modern silhouette—at the import stores in LA. I wished Michael had known more about what his sister meant by "traditional." Maybe he was more out of touch with his home culture than I'd realized.

The church was packed with friends and family. Nearly all the married women wore outfits of George fabric, brightly colored silk patterned with metallic thread, beading, crystals, and appliqué flowers, like the outfit Kate gave me before the wedding. I wished I had worn that outfit. Gele towered like skyscrapers. I'd never seen anything so glamorous.

After the short, solemn mass, we drove to a banquet hall for the post-memorial party. Many more people attended. Long foldout tables and folding chairs filled the room, with space at the front for dancing. A microphone was set up for speeches. In the kitchen at the back of the hall, huge aluminum pans held enormous amounts of chicken, beef, goat, jollof rice, stew, and pepper soup, which was way too spicy for me. Beer was plentiful.

Michael's eldest brother, John, began the gathering by talking about how important family was. Each spouse of an immediate family member was asked to come up to the microphone in the center of the room and state which family they represented.

John addressed the group in English out of regard for those of us who "had forgotten to learn Igbo," and a chuckle rose in the room.

Until that moment, I felt like I was stuck between cultures and had to choose: one that represented the Irish American father who raised me, and one that represented the black father I didn't know but who carried the key to my African American identity. Through Michael, I became part of a mixed-race British Nigerian family, where black, white, and mixed spouses were accepted with equal love along with a rainbow of cousins, nieces, and nephews. They were the surrogate mixed family I never had, comfortable in all the identities they represented, and cosmopolitan beyond my wildest dreams. But despite their hospitality, I didn't feel at home in London. I didn't catch the jokes and references and sometimes didn't understand their British accents. *They speak a lot faster than the British shows I watch on TV,* I thought. Some of the conversations included Igbo and pidgin, and Michael had to act as my translator. My Americanness set me apart, overriding our shared African and even mixed heritage.

Phil's turn came to declare her family ties, but she was shy and passed. Everyone knew and loved Phil, and no one took offense.

My turn was next. In front of me sat a sea of people of mostly Nigerian descent. It reminded me of standing in front of Mr. Lynch's World Cultures class but in reverse. I was the foreigner here, except this crowd was welcoming, and my difference was not a source of mockery. I could have passed and let the other family members continue their speeches, but I wanted to be seen.

"I am one of those who forgot to learn Igbo," I said. "So I will speak English. I am Sarah Valentine, and I represent the Dunn family of Pennsylvania and New Jersey in the United States." I told the crowd I was grateful to be part of the celebration and thanked them for welcoming me into their family.

As I walked back to my seat, Phil said, "What are you doing, making me look stupid!"

My family made me feel like my identity was an either-or decision. Now I realized it was possible to acknowledge the multiple families I held within me: the family that raised me, the family that embraced me, and the family I didn't know.

Thirty-nine

In the fall of 2012, Northwestern University's English department recruited Michael for an endowed professorship. Part of his incentive package was a permanent lectureship in the department for me. My contract with UC–Riverside expired at the end of the academic year, and though I went to a series of interviews at other universities, I did not get another position.

Part of UC–Riverside's counteroffer to keep Michael from leaving was a tenure-track position for me, but the offer would be void if Michael decided to accept the offer from Northwestern. We argued about what was best. I deserved the tenure-track position—I'd worked my whole life for it. But Northwestern's offer was better for him. I couldn't blame him; I would have taken the position, too.

Our relationship was already strained. Between his traveling and my erratic health, we grew apart. He turned to religion, and I met someone else. In the spring, we agreed to go to Evanston together though we were already separated. I didn't want to leave LA—I planned to make my life there—but other forces were pulling me forward.

Forty

Evanston, Illinois, a college town just north of Chicago, turned out to be beautiful. My apartment was a ten-minute walk from the university, which was on the coast of Lake Michigan. Parks, shops, and stately homes lined the streets. People jogged, pushed strollers, and walked dogs, sights rarely seen in LA. I taught creative writing in the English department as a visiting assistant professor. I'd chosen that position over a lectureship because at the time I didn't want to stay.

In October 2013, my brother Tom was getting married to Julie, who'd survived the Dunn gathering at Pop's funeral so well. A week or two before the wedding, I received a call from my aunt Liane, my mother's sister, whom I hadn't talked to since I was a kid.

"Dani gave me your number," she said, and I vaguely remembered my cousin, her daughter Dani, messaging me on Facebook for my contact details.

So many changes were happening in my life that I'd put the search for my biological father on hold. I got used to the idea of considering Gideon, the Kenyan in the photo, my father even though part of me knew it was a fantasy. My marriage was gone, the city I loved was gone, my friends had moved away. What did I have to hold on to? I felt more broken than ever and couldn't face more uncertainty.

"Your grandmother and I talked about it for a long time," she said, "but she didn't want to tell you. I think you have a right to know.

"I was worried about your mom when she went to college," Liane continued. "Her friends told me she was drinking, partying, and dating this strange guy. He was called the Prince, and he wore white robes."

"Was he African?" I asked. "Did he have an accent?"

"No," she said. "I think he was American. He even came to the house one day asking for her."

For the last eight years, my grandmother and aunt had debated whether or not to tell me about my biological father. My grandmother didn't reply when I sent Gideon's photo, and my grandfather must have known about his nickname.

So everyone knew. Everyone had known, including my mother, since before I was born.

"Do you know his real name?" I asked. "Was he a student?"

"I don't know," Liane said. "I just know his nickname was the Prince. When I went to campus to see her, to talk to her, she wasn't there. I don't know where she went."

"My mom never told me any of this," I said.

"I don't know when your mom became like she is," Liane said. "We haven't talked in a long time."

"She told me she was raped," I said.

"She never said anything about that," Liane replied.

The 1970s were a time of Afrocentrism, but it seemed like the detail of the Prince wearing white robes could be an exaggeration.

"Does anyone know his real name?" I asked.

She thought for a moment and then said, "Talk to Forbes. And Karen. She was your mom's roommate in college."

I saw Liane at my brother's wedding a few weeks later, but we didn't talk about what she'd told me. My mother was there, and I chose not to confront her about the version of her time in college that Liane gave me. After years of fighting, I knew it wouldn't change anything, and even if I pushed, I knew I would not get the answers I wanted. I finally followed Dr. Wade's advice and stayed in my square.

Over the next two years, I finished writing a book based on my dissertation. It also took me that long to work up the courage to contact Karen about the Prince and what happened to my mother that night. I found Karen on Facebook and contacted her through Instant Messenger.

She said there were two African American guys that she and my mother knew in college. One was the manager of the cafeteria where Karen and my mom worked for a few semesters. This was probably the same guy my mom mentioned when she'd revealed the story to me.

Karen described the cafeteria manager as "a very nice and good-looking man."

The other guy went by the name *the Prince*.

"No lie," Karen wrote. She said the Prince was also very good-looking. He was a smooth talker and sat with them often in the dining hall.

"He was very attentive to your mother," she wrote. She remembered that my mother had met up with him for the party, but Karen didn't go. She confirmed the Prince was an American student, not African. She remembered that my mother came back early the next morning, on her own, it seemed, and that she didn't talk about what had happened the previous night.

"Soon it was spring break," Karen wrote, "and she went to Florida with your dad and never returned to school. She was pregnant and I believe they got married in May."

Karen told me she knew how frustrating it must be for me not to know more, and she wished she had more information. But her loyalties remained with my parents.

"I love your mom and dad. They are wonderful people. Please do not mention this to them."

I'd been trying to contact Jimmy for six years, but I could never get ahold of him. I had seen that he had an account on Facebook and tried to friend him to no avail. Paranoid, I wondered if he was avoiding me. Now desperate, I tried him via his brother's email address, whom I'd contacted before. Two days later, I got a message in my in-box that included the lines:

Hey there Godchild; . . . the year/season you were conceived I had taken a semester off at WVU and was hitchhiking around our nation. So . . . I never laid eyes on the individual you're seeking out. However, a fellow (1974) classmate was there at the time. He knows! I'm not going to drag his name into your "unhealthy" endeavor, but I will contact him.

In the meantime, why don't you play P.I. and utilize the power of the internet by pulling up the 1976 football roster.

The yearbook for 1976 was not part of the university's digital database, so I tracked down a copy on eBay. I spent more than I should have on something most people probably threw away, reminders of the young people they no longer were, the cringeworthy styles they wore that dated them. They'd become different people with different lives, different needs and priorities. I felt the same way about my old high school yearbooks. Could I look at those photos and see who I was today?

In combing through yearbooks over thirty years old, I felt like I was chasing a person that no longer existed. Even if I found a name, a photograph, even an address somewhere online, where would that lead? Did I really want to know my biological father or just know about him? Did I prefer reality or fantasy?

I found the football team photos in the yearbook, but I still didn't know who I was looking for. Toward the end of the month, I received an email with the subject line: *Your request answered!*

Godchild: The name you are seeking is D. B. To the best of my pal's memory, he attended Valley High School in New Kensington, Pennsylvania (although not positive, 3 decades of rust).

It had been almost four decades, but I wasn't going to correct him. Instead, I ran back to the yearbooks and rosters and looked for the name. I found some stats for D. B. matching the years he'd played football.

I went to Classmates.com and found a Valley High School yearbook that contained D. B.'s photo. I checked back with Karen: Was this the name of the guy everyone knew as the Prince?

"WOW!" she wrote. "Where did you pull that name from?"

I told her that Jimmy's contact had told him, and Jimmy had passed it on to me.

Karen confirmed that yes, D. B. was the Prince, the same person my mom went to the party with that night.

I plugged D. B.'s name into search engines, but it was a common name and complicated by the fact that Karen remembered another first name associated with him, too. I tried all the variations I could, but got nothing beyond a high school yearbook photo and a few stats for a defensive tackle. It seemed he only played football for two years, and I could not find his picture among the senior class photos from 1976 to 1979. Could he have dropped out? I couldn't find a Facebook account or LinkedIn profile; or rather, since he had such a common name, I found too many of them. None matched the description of the person I was looking for.

I paid money to background-check search engines to see if I could find more detailed information. No hits—or rather, too many hits—in the databases of People Finder and Ancestry.com. Even with the internet's resources at my disposal, I could not find who I was looking for.

The next step, it seemed, was to hire a private detective, but I couldn't afford that and didn't know where to begin.

Forty-one

Susan grew up with my mother but went away to Georgetown for college. Through Facebook, I found out she lived near me in Wilmette, so we met up for drinks. The last time I'd seen Susan was at a Christmas party my parents threw over twenty years earlier.

She smiled when she saw me. "You look great!" she said. "I'd recognize you anywhere."

In the wake of the Rachel Dolezal scandal—the white woman who fooled people for years into thinking she was black—I wrote an article about my own experience with race and identity. I included a childhood photo of my brothers and me (and our cat) that showed our contrasting races.

When we sat down, Susan said, "I looked at the back page of *The Chronicle of Higher Education* and said, 'I know that photo!' Then I read the article and saw that you'd written it. It was so bizarre! You got your mother completely right—I could just hear her saying those things."

Because I found my mother's personality so combative, I asked Susan how they remained friends for so long.

"That's why I like her," she said. "She knows what she thinks and says it. She's always been that way."

My mother could be cheerful, insightful, compassionate, and funny, but I could never see her through the eyes of a lifelong friend. My mother and I had the same stubborn personalities and held opposing views. We cared deeply for each other, though unlike some mothers and daughters, we could never be friends.

I asked Susan if she knew that I was African American, and she said, "Yes. We knew from the day your mother brought you home."

I asked her, in frustration, why she and my mother's other friends never said anything.

"We didn't mostly out of respect for your dad."

So there it was. It had been an open secret to all my parents' family and friends, and probably all the friends and families I grew up with. Out of respect for my parents, perhaps particularly my father, no one brought it up.

But what about respect for me?

Both Karen and my aunt told me they thought I deserved to know. It was the reason they told me things that they did. For years, I was made to feel wrong while everyone around me protected my parents.

Forty-two

It was now more than ten years since I'd learned that the dad I grew up with was not my biological father and that I was a mixed-race African American.

It took years of costly therapy, antidepressants, and medical care, as well as physical, mental, emotional, and spiritual healing to reconstruct a self that could hold the trauma of transition, the painful incongruities of family and rape.

Maybe Jimmy was right that my quest was unhealthy.

My parents did try, in some ways, to adapt to my new sense of identity, but it didn't feel like enough, and I was angry that they didn't or couldn't try harder. When confessing this to Tara, she replied that my parents may not have the tools to deal with my transition the way that I could; that in this matter, they might never be able to give me what I want. She told me to go easy on them, but I was still too hurt. It seemed as though, even though they accepted that I was black now, they still saw our family as a white family; my mixed-race-ness was my issue alone and had nothing to do with them. I knew my transition was hurting them, too. It threw up a barrier between us, but I could not pretend that none of it ever happened, even if that was what they wanted.

The guilt tore me apart. Thoughts of oblivion crept in. Wouldn't it just be easier if I weren't here? I was in too much pain. We'd all be better off. I remembered a passage from David Mura's novel *Famous Suicides of the Japanese Empire*. Fujimoto plummets through the sky, his shadow looming larger and larger against the pavement as he falls. The only way to survive in this country, Mura writes, is to avoid memory, to live ghost-free. But I wanted my memories and the memories of my ancestors. I didn't want to survive by forsaking the past.

I wanted to find the original sickness: what made my mother the way she was; what made me the way I was. What we were experiencing had to be pathology. How could it be normal? If things were normal, I thought, none of it would have happened in the first place. My race wouldn't have been a secret. My father wouldn't have been the bogeyman.

Somehow, I knew it was all necessary, that I would have to endure the unmaking of myself before I could be whole again—if I even ever was—but I didn't know how long it would take, or if I could survive the unmaking.

After seeking multiple treatments without success, I was diagnosed with bipolar disorder II, the kind that tends toward depression. Bipolar disorder is hereditary, and in most cases, both parents suffer from it. With proper treatment, I started to feel like myself again: clearheaded and optimistic. I left my job at Northwestern and decided to make a new life for myself. I didn't know where I would end up, but I was open to all possibilities.

Forty-three

My mother's father died in the fall of 2016, and when I came home for Thanksgiving that year, she was editing together a slideshow of old family photos for the memorial service.

One showed her and her sister at five and six years old putting fluffy tinsel on a Christmas tree while their young, black-haired father in shirtsleeves sat on a nearby chair, smiling as he watched them.

"I look so sad in this photo," she said. I looked closer and saw that, indeed, the child in the photo did not look filled with wonder or holiday cheer. Her face was blank as she looked up at her smiling dad.

"Why?" I asked. "Do you remember what happened?"

She said nothing, and then, vaguely, "I don't know."

In another photo of her father as a young man, she cropped the cigarette he was holding out of the photo.

"Why did you do that, Mom?" I asked. My grandfather smoked through most of his adult life, only quitting when his health required it.

"Because this is how I want it. This is how it should have been."

Back in LA when I began writing a memoir, Claire suggested I read Paul Auster's memoir *The Invention of Solitude*. After reading it, I realized how much writing can be about not writing; what happens when we come to emotionally difficult places that make our pencils stop and hover over the paper, our fingers pause above the keys. Those moments make us stand up, get some coffee, look out the window, check emails, clean the kitchen, file papers, pay bills, make phone calls, eat cookies, pace endlessly, or leave us staring off into space until we realize we can't place the moment our minds began to wander, what we were thinking about, how long we've been sitting. We realize we are crying and cannot remember how or why it began.

We build up fantasies little by little every day until they become a story we can live with. Things are smoothed over, and inconvenient bumps—the ones that lead down roads to things that are even more terrifying—are edited out.

In Auster's memoir, he realized his family's amnesia about his grandfather and how he died was actually hiding a dark family secret—the fact that his grandmother murdered him. His father's strangely distant behavior became illuminated, if not fully explained, by his role in these events as a boy, who, at five years old, was called to witness in court about his father's murder. The grandfather's image had been ripped out of family photos, which were taped back together as if he had never existed. His family altered the narrative of their lives to protect itself, to create a story they could live with. It was never spoken of and was probably carried out in bits and pieces, unconsciously, over time. The subject was ignored until it ceased to exist.

In 2012, Michael and I traveled to Mantua, Italy, for a literary festival. We flew to Bologna and were met at the airport by volunteers from the Mantua Literature Festival—Franco, a retired driver who we soon learned had been working the festival for fourteen years, and Francesca, an eighteen-year-old who spoke Italian, Spanish, French, and English and wanted to learn Chinese. She chatted amicably with us as we headed north and west and soon we found ourselves traveling through a serene countryside studded with crumbling farmhouses.

The sunset cast an orange glow over the fields, and it began to sink in that I was in the country of my ancestors. I was surrounded by Renaissance architecture lit up against a blue night sky so that the edge of every brick and dark window stood out. Suddenly, I felt the weight, the urgency, of the past.

My grandfather's family was from a small town called San Pietro, but there are dozens of San Pietros in Italy, and the family's best guess is that it is the one in central Italy, near Rome.

I have vague memories of those Italian relatives from the only family reunion we ever had. I was young, maybe nine or ten, and remember people who were very old, especially my Japanese great-aunt, whom my great-uncle brought home from the war. My mother seemed to be there out of a sense of duty. I don't think my grandfather attended the reunion.

Even from the family I know, all I have are fragments.

I'll never know the whole story of what happened between my mother and D. B. Because my mother was working through long-buried trauma for the first time, every time she told me the story it was different. Maybe she wasn't drugged; maybe she just drank too much. Sometimes the story had no rape, just a blank page of memory.

Eventually, she settled on the account that someone wronged her.

"I realized what it was," she told me, "when I saw a story on the news about a girl who had been raped while passed out and the incident had been recorded on a cell phone. That could have been me,

I thought. If there were cell phones back when it happened, that could have been me."

As time went on, I started to understand that the search for my biological father was important to me because I never felt authentically black. I thought I needed him to prove something that the people around me made me question my whole life. I felt like an imposter, and I thought finding my father would cure that. I wanted someone I could point to and say, "See? I was right all along."

I came to realize that even with the holes in my family tree, the trauma of my conception, and the feeling of incompleteness that comes from being cut off from half my ancestry, I am enough. My looks, my background, my experiences, and inner world are enough. There is no standard experience of mixed-ness or blackness: there are as many ways to be black or mixed as there are black or mixed people in the world.

On a recent visit home, I asked my parents what it was like growing up in the 1960s and 1970s, during desegregation and the civil rights movement. Even if they were young, surely they remembered the assassinations of JFK and MLK Jr., the Freedom Riders, the bra burnings, the student demonstrations on college campuses.

My father said he watched the Watts riots on TV in 1965 and saw black people looting and destroying their own neighborhoods. He was about ten years old. He didn't understand why they would do something like that.

He told me about Mr. Good, an old black man who hung out at a café where he played pinball as a kid and who would talk to him and tell him stories. He talked about Greg Morris on *Mission: Impossible* and Bill Cosby on *I Spy*, well-educated blacks in the media whom he looked up to.

"Those were the people who were role models," he said.

My mother said that, as a kid, she didn't pay attention to what was going on around her. She said she vaguely understood that people were being oppressed and that it was wrong. She said she never heard her father use the N-word. Instead, he would talk about the "shanty Irish" and the "lace curtain Irish." She didn't mention any specific memories, news, or events from the civil rights era. Because she is a pro-life feminist, I thought she'd mention *Roe v. Wade,* Title IX, or the women's rights movement. If she didn't know Angela Davis, at least she would know Gloria Steinem. I asked her about this, and all she said, shaking her head, was, "I was stupid."

It seemed that none of the conflicts of that time touched my parents personally. Racial injustice was something that happened to other people in other parts of the country. I wondered how differently whites and blacks of that generation, the baby boomers, experienced that era.

My father did a DNA test that proved he was 75 percent Irish.

"More Irish than the Irish!" he said, noting that according to the test, people who have lived in Ireland for generations are only 72 percent Irish. He talked of his desire to take my brothers on a heritage trip to Ireland so they could see where their ancestors came from. He left me out of the invitation, acknowledging tacitly that I do not, in fact, have a genetic link to his family, yet not offering any sign that my past might matter, too.

The accuracy of ancestry DNA tests became more refined in the ten years since I took my first test in 2006. The results from my recent test from Ancestry.com came back:

39 percent Italian
45 percent West and Central African (Cameroon, Congo, Benin/Togo, Southern Bantu, Ivory Coast/Ghana, and Mali)

8 percent Russian

8 percent West and Northern European (England/Wales,
   Baltic and Germanic regions)

1 percent Native American

The most recent large-scale migrations for my ancestors, around 1860, were from Southern Italy, Virginia, and the Southern United States. Southern Italians traveled to the United States to escape desperate poverty called *la miseria* in their newly unified country. At the same time, almost half of all enslaved African Americans lived in Virginia. After emancipation, black families spread throughout the Black Belt, the fertile region sweeping the Carolinas, Georgia, Alabama, Mississippi, Louisiana, and Texas to work the land as sharecroppers. In the Great Migration African Americans moved to the North, Midwest, and West Coast. While I know my mother's European ancestors came to this country around the turn of the twentieth century, my African American ancestors had probably already been in this country for four hundred years.

The eight percent Russian surprised me. Maybe, as my grandfather insisted, we do have Cossacks in our family.

I have been to Rome, the Vatican, Florence, Mantua, Turin, and Palermo, but except for a three-day conference in New Orleans, I have never been to the South. Every week or so, I get notifications about new relatives on Ancestry.com, most of them distant, most of them African Americans. One man was listed as my second cousin or first cousin once removed. His family came from North Carolina. We could not find our common ancestor, but those answers are out there. I still have a long, fruitful journey ahead of me.

Forty-four

Looking back through old emails with my mother from 2006, I was struck by how cooperative she was being, or was trying to be, at the time. She said she was ready to go to counseling, ready to do whatever was necessary to help me through that rough time. I was complaining about not getting interviews and jobs while my white colleagues did. My mother was upset on my behalf and asked if I should contact the ACLU.

My parents tried to meet me halfway during my journey, but that was the problem: I didn't want to meet halfway. I wanted to meet on my terms because I was too angry and hurt. I felt like I had lived my whole life by their terms and the terms of all our friends and family that wanted to protect my parents from the reality they'd created. I love my parents, and I know they love me, but I live on my own terms now.

Racism runs deep, even in people who don't consider themselves racist. Any time I leveled that accusation against my parents they felt wrongfully attacked. But what else could you call it? Whiteness was protecting itself at my expense, and the racism lay in assuming that blackness and race were things my parents needed to be protected from. They should have known better, and maybe they did. Maintaining whiteness in the service of white supremacy turns people into cowards.

I don't know where my parents fall on the spectrum of white racial identity development, but I don't think they have integrated their whiteness into an awareness of structural racism. Or maybe, as with my racial identity, they knew about their role in upholding a society that grants them privilege but were never forced to confront it. I've learned that even when white people are forced to confront race and racism, it's easy for them to turn way.

My brother Tom and his wife, Julie, live in a house near my parents and have two adorable sons. Their black Lab, Pepper, is rambunctious but better behaved than cake-stealing Knight. Tom has always been supportive of me and speaks out against white supremacy when family arguments arise. I hope his sons take advantage of his and Julie's wisdom and grow up with a broader, more inclusive worldview than we did.

Years after the revelation, I wrote to Tom asking what he remembered from that day. I remembered that he was mostly quiet then, and though he expressed his unconditional support for me afterward, we had never talked about what happened.

"I drove with Mommy/Daddy from Pittsburgh to Princeton, sitting in the back seat, and I remember it being cold/snowy," he wrote.

When we got closer to Princeton—maybe about an hour away—I remember the silence being broken by Mommy with a line along the lines of "there is something we need to tell you about Sarah." The story started with something like "when we were in college before Daddy and I were dating or married, something happened" and I